NO HOLIER
SPOT OF
GROUND

NO HOLIER SPOT OF GROUND

CONFEDERATE MONUMENTS & CEMETERIES OF SOUTH CAROLINA

KRISTINA DUNN JOHNSON

Charleston — London

THE
History
PRESS

Published by The History Press
Charleston, SC 29403
www.historypress.net

Copyright © 2009 by Kristina Dunn Johnson
All rights reserved

First published 2009
Second printing 2010

Manufactured in the United States

ISBN 978.1.59629.397.7

Library of Congress Cataloging-in-Publication Data

Johnson, Kristina Dunn.
No holier spot of ground : Confederate monuments and cemeteries of South Carolina /
Kristina Dunn Johnson.
p. cm.
ISBN 978-1-59629-397-7
1. South Carolina--History--Civil War, 1861-1865--Monuments. 2. United States-
-History--Civil War, 1861-1865--Monuments. 3. Cemeteries--South Carolina. 4.
Soldiers' monuments--South Carolina. 5. War memorials--South Carolina. 6. Historical
markers--South Carolina. 7. Soldiers' monuments--Southern States. I. Title.
E645J645 2009
973.7'6--dc22
2009004389

Dedicated in memory of
Elizabeth Fox-Genovese
and
Rebecca A. Lyons

Thank you both for your loving encouragement.
Your mentorship has made me a better person and historian.

"Ode to Magnolia Cemetery"

Sleep gently in your humble graves,
Sleep martyrs of a fallen cause;
Though yet no marble column craves,
The pilgrim here to pause.

In the seeds of laurel in the earth
The blossom of your fame is blown,
And somewhere waiting for its birth,
The shaft is in the stone.

Meanwhile, behalf your tardy years
Which in trust keep your storied tombs,
Behold! your sisters bring their tears,
And these memorial blooms.

Small tributes! but your shades will smile
More proudly on these wreaths today,
Than when some cannon-moulded pile
Shall overlook this bay.

Stoop angels, hither from the skies!
There is no holier spot of ground
Than where defeated valor lies,
By mourning beauty crowned!

CONTENTS

ACKNOWLEDGEMENTS

The beginnings of this book started when I was in high school, when my parents agreed to take me to Civil War battlefields on spring break instead of the beach. Visiting Gettysburg, Appomattox, Manassas, Sharpsburg and other battlefields, I snapped pictures of all the Confederate monuments that I saw, not yet fully understanding their meaning. And, although my brother complained about how every battlefield looked the same, even he is now intrigued by the stories of the war and its legacy. Mom, Dad, PJ—I can never thank you enough for all of your support.

I could not have written this book without the loving support of my husband, Tommy. He stuck with me through all my episodes of writer's block and kept pushing me toward this goal. He became an invaluable research assistant, helping with pictures and finding interesting stories. This book is greatly enhanced by having him in my life.

Additionally, Gordon Jones at the Atlanta History Center played a critical role in the development of this book by teaching me the importance of the "myth and memory" of the war. I hope that I do justice to the topic of monumentation in your home state! Thank you for teaching me about the importance of understanding the historiography of the war's legacies.

I would be remiss not to thank the supportive staff of the South Carolina Confederate Relic Room and Military Museum: Allen Roberson, Sarah W. Garrod, Joe Long, Jai Cassidy-Shaiman, Rachel Cockrell, John Bigham and Shirley Schoonover. I am proud to work alongside all of you. Thank you for your help with this project and letting me bounce ideas off of you. I also appreciate the support of the Gettysburg National Military Park during my time there, especially the friendship and research assistance of Terry Latschar, John Latschar, Troy Harman, Becky Lyons, Greg Coco, Winona Peterson, Kathy Georg Harrison, Linda Neylon, Janet Bucklew, Scott Hartwig and John Heiser. Gratitude is also due to John Sherrer, Kaela Harmon, Ann

Posner, Jackie Rhodes and Robin Waites, who supported me during my work at Historic Columbia Foundation.

The efforts of the South Carolina Division of the Sons of Confederate Veterans and the United Daughters of the Confederacy have been invaluable. Thank you for patiently listening and providing insight to my talks on Confederate monuments and cemeteries. I tried to incorporate as many of your stories as I could, but I was unable to include everything. I would especially like to thank the members of SCV Palmetto Camp #22 in Columbia; SCV H.L. Hunley Camp #143 in Summerville; SCV Brigadier General Samuel McGowan Camp #40 in Laurens; UDC Mary Boykin Chesnut Chapter #2517 in Columbia; and UDC Ellison Capers Chapter #70 in Florence. Especially helpful were Frank Berry, Dean Stevens, Ashley Stevens, Tom Elmore, Krys Wood-Elmore, Robert Roper III, Gary Davis, Nita Keisler and Kevin Lassen. I am also indebted to the earlier work done by the UDC Wade Hampton Chapter #29 in Columbia while it oversaw the Confederate Relic Room collection. Please continue to preserve and protect your local monuments and cemeteries.

I appreciate the support of the Emory History Department and the University of South Carolina History Department while I researched topics surrounding the development of the memory and legacy of the Civil War, especially Elizabeth Fox-Genovese, Paige Putnam-Miller and Thomas Brown.

Thanks is also due to the research assistance and support given to me by Lindsay Pettus, Louise Pettus, James Clary, Dale Molina, Robert W. Foster, Garry Adelman, Neill Rose, Jennifer Scheetz of the Charleston Museum, Mike Coker at the South Carolina Historical Society, Robin Copp of the South Caroliniana Library, Donna Alley of the Beaufort Planning Department, Susie Baier at Elmwood Cemetery, Eric Emerson at the Charleston Library, Ann Evans of the Springs Close Family Archives (the White Homestead) and Wade Dorsey and Patrick McCauley at the South Carolina Department of Archives and History. The staff of Beaufort National Cemetery was also very helpful. I appreciate all of the work done by Robert Seigler in his earlier book to catalogue all of the Confederate monuments in the state. I would also like to thank Dan Gidick for connecting me with The History Press. I appreciate the assistance of my editor, Laura All, and the staff of The History Press for getting this book to the public.

"NO HOLIER SPOT OF GROUND"

As Henry Timrod, the "Poet Laureate of the Confederacy," read his "Ode to Magnolia Cemetery" during the 1867 Memorial Day services at Charleston's Magnolia Cemetery, he could not have foretold just how many "marble columns" would someday grace the Southern landscape. During a time when many Southerners were attempting to cope with defeat and gather their dead, Timrod recognized an underlying desire to create permanent memorials to the tragedy. His words inspired the gathered crowd and reminded them that after the immediacy of mourning, memorialization would help future generations remember the South's pain and sacrifice.

This book endeavors to tell South Carolina's story of Confederate memorialization through establishing burial arrangements and monuments. It is intended to remind the general public of the importance of monumentation, and how it changed through time. In their rush to explore broad cultural patterns and sociopolitical meanings, many historians become consumed in evaluating abstract details and writing in difficult-to-understand language. Unfortunately, all too frequently, some historians forget that they are studying real people with real emotions. The wartime death of a son, brother or husband provoked the same emotional reactions as a death would today—sorrow, anger, questioning and the desire for closure. These were Americans coping with genuine loss. Such sentiments cannot be underestimated, especially among the generation that endured the hardships of the Confederate War. Certainly, commemorating their deaths and service became embedded within larger social and political meanings. This book will attempt to explore those meanings without forgetting about the humanity involved in the process.

The shadow of loved ones lost during the war haunted thousands of households across America. Approximately 620,000 Northern and Southern men died during four years of bloody conflict. The presence of death was nearly suffocating, especially in the South, where combat or disease killed one in three Confederate soldiers. In the Palmetto State alone, nearly 21,000 military men died out of the approximately 63,000 troops mustered into service. Each number within this astounding death total directly represents an individual whose life came to a tragically short end, leaving behind unfulfilled hopes and dreams. Likewise, it also represents the families whose worlds were instantly shattered. Never again would they feel the embrace, hear the laugh or experience the comfort of their loved one. Additionally, thousands of families throughout the country were unable to reclaim their soldier's remains—many never learned their loved ones' exact fate on the battlefield or within the prison camps. The psychological impact of such a devastating loss cannot be underestimated when attempting to understand the primary motivations behind Southern memorialization.

Along with this emotional devastation caused by wartime death, a severe economic depression and Radical Republican governments invaded the South. Many Northerners desired to reprimand the South for its betrayal of the Union, and thus attempted to impose punitive political and economic measures. Radical Republicans espoused the most ardent measures of retribution against the former Confederate states and Southerners responded with a mix of anxiety and anger. The political atmosphere of the Reconstruction era forced former Confederates to retreat and mourn together in private locations. During these years, Southerners began to form communal outpourings of tangible symbols of grief and memory, such as monuments. Not until after Wade Hampton's election, however, would South Carolinians venture into public courthouse squares to commemorate and vindicate their dead.

Monuments represent an outpouring of community cohesiveness. In stone and bronze, society decided on a particular message to impart to future generations concerning the nature and legacy of the Confederate War. As Bishop Ellison Capers poignantly extolled at the dedication of the South Carolina monument at Chickamauga,

> *Public monuments are the recognized symbols of worthy history. They are enduring exponents of character. The lessons which high example and honorable history teach are written not alone in the perishable pages of books, or in the fading memories of a generation. True patriotism has ever engraven them in stone, and builded high their immortality in granite and Parian marble.*[1]

"No Holier Spot of Ground"

Confederate monumentation in South Carolina began as a communal way to mourn the dead, but it transformed into a political statement of resistance toward the North. Around the turn of the twentieth century, monumentation started to shift from a defiant political statement and instead focus on the common experience shared by white Southerners and Northerners during the war. Monumentation throughout South Carolina can be broken down into four distinct phases: Reconstruction, 1865–77; post-Reconstruction and Southern vindication, 1878–1903; nationalism and the Lost Cause, 1904–22; and modern remembrances, 1923–present.

Furthermore, cemeteries contain messages about the importance of the war dead. Victorian culture sentimentalized death and established new ideas concerning appropriate burial arrangements with specialized mourning rituals. Therefore, every aspect of Victorian-era death was imbedded with intended, explicit meaning. These patterns were disrupted during the war, but both sides attempted to uphold to Christian burial arrangements and ideas of patriotic sacrifice. North and South alike selected burial arrangements that reflected larger ideas of the war and the country, which created unique and enduring expressions within local communities. Additionally, the finality of death gave a sense of permanence to messages imparted through burial arrangements. As one Union veteran stated, "Established, ornamented, and forever the objects of national care and protection, they [national cemeteries] will become so many ineffaceable historical records."[2] Therefore, the significance of these cemeteries will ensure that larger messages surrounding the war will also endure for generations.

This book attempts to weave together a narrative of how South Carolinians united to create memorials to the Confederate dead and vindicate the Confederate Cause. This book is not intended to provide a listing and history of each Confederate monument or cemetery within the Palmetto State. Robert Seigler's *"Passing the Silent Cup": A Guide to Confederate Monuments in South Carolina* provides an excellent listing of Confederate monuments throughout South Carolina. This work will hopefully serve as a companion to Seigler's guide by establishing a narrative and chronology of South Carolina Confederate monumentation. Furthermore, it will include the creation of wartime burial sections and monuments outside of the state's physical boundaries.

It would also be impossible to list every cemetery in South Carolina that holds the remains of Confederate or Union soldiers, especially considering that an overall burial index does not currently exist. In order to fill this gap, the South Carolina Division of the Sons of Confederate Veterans is presently compiling an inventory of Confederate soldiers buried within the state. However, six South Carolina cemeteries serve as case studies for this book: Magnolia Cemetery in Charleston; Elmwood Cemetery in Columbia; Springwood Cemetery in Greenville; St. David's Episcopal Church burial ground in Cheraw; Mount Hope Cemetery in Florence; and Beaufort National Cemetery. Although a Union cemetery, Beaufort National Cemetery uniquely decided to include wartime Confederate burials in its boundaries.

This work will focus on burial and monumentation patterns that can be applied to cemeteries across the state. Hopefully, readers of this book will become more aware of the characteristics of monuments and cemeteries throughout the South, but especially in the Palmetto State. Previous generations of Southerners committed enormous amounts of time and resources in order to permanently impart the depth of their loss and their commitment to the Confederate Cause. Subsequently, it can be seen how each generation was influenced by its closeness to the war, the legacy of Reconstruction, Lost Cause ideology and national events.

Unfortunately, many of the messages of previous generations are lost to the current generation. Consumed with talking on their cellphones or blaring the radio, people zoom past monuments, barely even noting their existence. Modern culture has disengaged with its surrounding environment, especially those things not extraordinarily flashy. Sadly, as time passes and new generations are not educated in the classics, Victorian and Christian symbolism seem abstract. Hopefully, if the present generation is reminded of the humanity and sacrifices of the generation who fought in the war, our culture will be more inclined to preserve and protect important cultural sites and artifacts.

In 1903, Margaret Crawford Adams of Conagree, South Carolina, the wife of a Confederate soldier, already recognized an emerging disconnect between the contemporary generation and her wartime experience. She was compelled to impart the tragedy of the war to those who would listen. Adams touchingly reminisced to her grandchildren:

> No mail came without bringing sad news to some home, and the telegraph wires would flash the report of the deaths of hundreds and thousands of loved ones, who had lost their lives for the "Cause." You go to a funeral now, dear children; the solemn burial services is read in a church; mourning friends follow the beloved form to the grave, and put it away with all the tenderness of the human heart. Do you think such was the burial of our brave, dead soldiers? Ah! no! no! Some there were whose mortal remains were brought home in rude coffins, and now rest in peaceful churchyards or

cemeteries, and year by year you go with those who strew their graves with garlands and flowers, and thus keep green their memories; but thousands fill unknown graves; thousands were piled in heaps together, without even the poor blanket wrapped around them, for a winding sheet; some were blown to atoms, and no trace left of them; hundreds languished and perished in Northern prisons.[3]

This is the story of some of these men and the inheritance their loved ones entrusted us with as they attempted to cope with the legacy of the war.

CHAPTER 1

"THOUSANDS FILL UNKNOWN GRAVES"

Wartime Burials

I reached here yesterday evening with the remains of Tallie [sic]. *He was buried upon the battlefield about a half mile from where he was killed…The boys buried Capt Williams & Tally in the same grave, and they were taken up together…I procured for his body a quite handsomely finished oak coffin in Atlanta and hope it will reach you in good condition. His blanket was carefully put around him, and we placed him in his coffin without unfolding it at all. I suppose it is unnecessary to advise you not to open it, but for fear some of the family might desire it done, I would say* don't do it. *He had been buried one week when I reached the grave.*
—*Captain Harry P. Farrow to Richard Franklin Simpson, Tally's father, on September 29, 1863*[4]

It was news that no family wished to receive—the Simpson family's beloved son, Taliaferro (Tally), had been killed at the Battle of Chickamauga, fighting alongside his comrades in the Third South Carolina Infantry. Nevertheless, the Simpson family was fortunate to know Tally's ultimate fate and to be able to immediately retrieve his remains for reburial. This fact, however, provided only a small measure of comfort to a grieving family coping with the heart-wrenching knowledge that their loved one was never returning home.

The grim realities of horrific battlefield deaths, agonizing fatal wounds and un-Christian burial arrangements did not escape the notice of the soldiers. Additionally, soldiers were constantly reminded of the possibility of leaving families behind to cope with their deaths. After witnessing the Battle of Fredericksburg in December of 1862, Tally wrote to his sister, Anna:

> *This day, one year ago, how many thousand families, gay and joyous, celebrating Merry Christmas, drinking health to the absent members of their family, and sending upon the wings of love and affection long, deep,*

and sincere wishes for their safe return to the loving ones at home, but today are clad in the deepest mourning in memory to some lost and loved member of their circle. If all the dead (those killed since the war began) could be heaped in one pile and all the wounded be gathered together in one group, the pale faces of the dead and the groans of the wounded would send such a thrill of horror through the hearts of the originators of this war that their very souls would rack with such pain that they would prefer being dead and in torment than to stand before God with such terrible crimes blackening their characters. Add to this the cries and wailings of the mourners—mothers and fathers weeping for their sons, sisters for their brothers, wives for their husbands, and daughters for their fathers—how deep would be the convictions of their consciences.

Tally's family, like many others, would spend their next Christmas in "the deepest mourning," as he would be killed within the next year.[5]

At the Battle of Chickamauga in September of 1863, the Third South Carolina Infantry was ordered to charge Snodgrass Hill. During the fierce assault, Tally and his fellow comrade, Captain Albert "Putts" Williams, were instantly killed. In the wake of the battle, their comrades buried Tally and Putts in a single grave. The two men shared the grave for several days before being forever separated and carried home to their families in South Carolina. Ironically, both of their fathers had been signers of the Ordinance of Secession. Putts was reburied in his family's plot in the Laurens town cemetery. Meanwhile, Tally was reburied in the Simpson family cemetery on the peaceful, rolling farmland outside of Pendleton—a stark contrast to the shallow and hasty battlefield graves where many of his fellow Confederates remained for years after the war. Appropriately, in 1901, a South Carolina monument would be dedicated on the battlefield in the shadow of Snodgrass Hill, where the soldiers fought and sacrificed for the Southern Cause.[6]

As evidenced by Tally's letters and his grieving family, South Carolina civilians quickly began to comprehend the human cost of the war. The chaos created by battlefield death and lack of communication produced disarray on the homefront. Mrs. Williams of Pendleton later remembered, "Every battle brought its list of dead and dying to our village, when at last its fatal results were known, and one by one each home within its borders was desolated. Ill news came heralded by signals well understood. Loud, prolonged, and piercing screams…broke the stillness of the night."

In too many instances, families did not know if a loved one was killed, captured or wounded after a battle. Often, families frantically searched wounded lists only to be disappointed by the ambiguous term "missing."

Taliaferro "Tally" Simpson, killed at the Battle of Chickamauga. *Courtesy of South Carolina Confederate Relic Room and Military Museum and Ed and Maureen Simpson.*

Washington Albert "Putts" Williams, who shared a grave with Tally Simpson for several days on the battlefield before their remains were separated and transported home. Putts was reburied in the Laurens town cemetery. *Courtesy of South Carolina Confederate Relic Room and Military Museum, Isabel W. Foster and John W. Foster.*

The final resting place of Tally Simpson outside of Pendleton, South Carolina. In 1992, members of the Simpson family erected a monument in his honor beside his original headstone. Tally's father, an Ordinance of Secession signer, is buried next to him. *Courtesy of Kristina and Tommy Johnson.*

Unable to care for their own dead or wounded relatives, many Southern civilians poured their emotions into sending care packages, engaging in fundraisers or caring for the ill and wounded recovering in nearby hospitals.[7]

In the Palmetto State, death soon came riding the trains from distant battlefields in Virginia and from nearby siege fighting around Charleston and Savannah. Towns along the rail lines, such as Columbia, Florence, Charleston, Camden, Greenville and Pendleton, quickly became inundated with wounded and ill soldiers who were too unstable to continue on their journeys. To alleviate the situation, Ladies Aid Societies established wayside hospitals at train stations as well as semipermanent hospitals within the towns. Eventually, the Confederate army established permanent, government-run hospitals in main cities along the railway while the towns formalized systems of burying the dead.

Unfortunately, when the trains pulled out of the station, often any hope of comrades revealing the identities of these men also departed. Even when away from the battlefield, many of these soldiers died in anonymity simply by being too weak or delusional to state their own names. Explaining the situation in 1901, Mrs. Joseph Marshall of Abbeville recalled a Confederate soldier with smallpox: "In a few days he died, never able to tell his name. He was buried near the house in which he died, and a cedar tree, planted by a little girl, is all that marks the resting place of, no doubt, a true and brave soldier."[8] Constrained by wartime circumstances, the citizens of Abbeville could do little more for the soldier.

In Columbia, the young ladies of the city had established a wayside hospital at the rail depot on Gervais Street. At the outset, as in other towns, those soldiers too ill to continue traveling were taken to houses around Columbia to recuperate. By the winter of 1861–62, the ladies of the city had organized a temporary hospital at the Fair Grounds. Notwithstanding their best efforts, Mrs. Campbell Bryce reported, "During the winter following, some forty soldiers died, many from pneumonia, some from typhoid fever, and others from erysipelas." After the winter, the Confederate army finally established a permanent base hospital in the city, located at the South Carolina College Horseshoe.[9]

Meanwhile, a portion of Elmwood Cemetery was established as a Confederate burial section. Founded in 1854, Elmwood Cemetery reflected the Victorian landscape cemetery movement of utilizing cemeteries as parks outside of the main city limits. Organizers of the cemetery included prominent South Carolinians such as General Wade Hampton III and William Glaze of the Palmetto Armory. When Sherman's troops came through Columbia in February of 1865, the records of Elmwood Cemetery were sent to the Washington Street Methodist Church for safekeeping. Although the cemetery escaped damage, Union troops burned the church, resulting in the destruction of the early cemetery records. Some of the destroyed information included records about the establishment and burials in the Confederate section of the cemetery. A letter from the Ladies Memorial Association in 1866 lamented the fire and the loss of records, implying that some of the identities of these unknown soldiers went up in the inferno of February 17, 1865.[10]

According to an inventory compiled around the turn of the century, approximately 261 soldiers were interred in the Confederate section between 1862 and 1865. Of these soldiers, 141 were unknown either at the time of their death or by the time the list was created. Initially, wooden planks marked the burial location and displayed known information for each soldier. These wooden headboards were replaced in 1924, after the aforementioned list was created, with small, square stone markers. Some of these small stones can

Elmwood Cemetery prior to the placement of new headstones in 1985. *Courtesy of South Carolina Confederate Relic Room and Military Museum.*

still be seen today. In 1985, only 174 graves were recognizable, resulting in the loss of 87 graves. With the help of the South Carolina National Guard, the South Carolina Civil War Roundtable replaced the headstones with standard Confederate grave markers provided by the United States Veterans Administration.[11] Recent counts place the overall number of Confederate burials throughout Elmwood Cemetery at more than 500 soldiers and veterans, including a female spy and 2 Confederate generals.

Greenville experienced similar challenges as the state capital. Just as in Columbia, the ladies of Greenville organized a Confederate hospital. In order to cope with the dead soldiers who could not be returned to their own hometowns, Springwood Cemetery established a Confederate section. During the war, eighty Confederate soldiers would be laid to rest in this section—far from home, but at least buried in Dixie.[12]

As demonstrated by the earlier story of Tally Simpson and Putts Williams, those soldiers who died on the battlefield had a far different experience of death and burial than those who died in Southern hospitals. The logistical difficulties involved with burying thousands of bodies in the wake of a major battle overwhelmed army orderlies and local civilians. They simply could not

Elmwood Cemetery as it appears today. *Courtesy of Tommy Johnson.*

Confederate burials at Springwood Cemetery in Greenville. *Courtesy of Kristina and Tommy Johnson.*

keep up with identifying, organizing and properly burying soldiers' remains. In the best of circumstances, each soldier within a trench would receive his own burial shroud and a wooden headboard hastily marked with his identity. Most soldiers did not receive such dignified care.

The Union government solved the problem of mass wartime burials through the establishment and financing of national cemeteries. This system allowed Federal soldiers to be reburied in permanent cemeteries during and immediately after the war. Confederates were usually not allowed to be buried in these national cemeteries, especially during the war. Such was the case after the famous battle on Pennsylvania soil. At Gettysburg, the task of reburying the Union dead in a permanent national cemetery began just a few months after the fighting. The Confederate dead, however, were purposely left in their shallow trench graves on the battlefield for years to come. Samuel Weaver, the Federal government contractor for the reinterment process, assured the government that they had successfully completed the task of reburial in the national cemetery with the strict guidelines of not including Confederate remains. Weaver proudly reported:

> *It may be asked how we could distinguish the bodies of our own men from those of the rebels. This was generally very easily done...In no instance*

was a body allowed to be removed which had any portion of rebel clothing on it. Taking all of these things together, we never had much trouble in deciding, with infallible accuracy, whether the body was that of a Union soldier or a rebel. And I here most conscientiously assert, that I firmly believe that there has not been a single mistake made in the removal of the soldiers to the cemetery by taking the body of a rebel for a Union soldier.[13]

Federal government funds paid Weaver $1.59 for each soldier's remains that he was able to identify as a Union soldier for reburial in the national cemetery. Although nearly half of their names were unknown, Weaver located 3,512 remains that he identified as Federal soldiers. Later research demonstrated that at least 9 of these men were actually Confederate soldiers. In November of 1863, these reburied soldiers were forever immortalized in Lincoln's famous Gettysburg Address. While this widely heralded event took place, Confederates remained decomposing in shallow graves in nearby fields.[14]

Afterward, Gettysburg civilians were left to maintain the Confederate graves that remained on their property. The townspeople expressed various

Confederate dead on the Gettysburg battlefield. This image was taken near the Rose Farm, where many South Carolinians of Kershaw's Brigade fought and died. *Courtesy of Library of Congress.*

reactions to these Confederate dead. Some citizens treated them reverently and cared for the remains as fellow Christians and Americans. Other farmers protested to the Federal government to rebury the dead in a permanent cemetery so that crop fields could be regained. Less scrupulous individuals plowed through the graves and used the headboards as firewood in order to survive the wartime winters.[15]

On February 2, 1864, the *Star-Sentinel* reported:

> *There appears to be considerable feeling in and around Gettysburg, that a place be set apart for the burial of the Confederate dead who are now buried promiscuously over the battlefield, or in the vicinity. The recent rains have washed the places where they are buried, which, in a short time the land will be put under cultivation, and not a trace of their last resting place will be left. Common humanity would dictate a removal to some spot, not in or about our National Cemetery, but the purchase of ground somewhere, where Southern friends may, when the rebellion is crushed, and all in peace, make their pilgrimage here. Our State should not make the purchase, nor should it be expected; but if Southern people should express the desire and would carry it to completion, we should say—let it be done for the sake of our common humanity.[16]*

Although the editorial did not recommend the possible logistics for enacting such a plan, it exposed a larger desire for a permanent solution for the Confederate dead out of necessity and basic humanity. Mercifully, Dr. John W.C. O'Neal of Gettysburg embarked upon a mission to locate, identify and map the Confederate burial sites and reconcile those with available military and hospital records. In 1866, his work culminated in a list of Confederate burial locations that he hoped would help Southern families reclaim their dead loved ones. Unfortunately, it was not until 1871, eight years after the battle, that the first reburial of Confederate soldiers occurred.[17]

Like civilians living in Gettysburg, South Carolinians also soon experienced the difficult pressures of the battlefield colliding with the homefront. In addition to caring for the Confederates that arrived by train, an influx of dying and wounded swept through the region in early 1865, as General William Tecumseh Sherman's troops cut a swath of destruction through the Carolinas. This increase of casualties and the uncertainty created by the Yankee invasion fostered new pressures and trials. South Carolinians worried about safekeeping their property, maintaining food sources and protecting their families. Additionally, civilians became apprehensive about the security of graveyards of Southerners who had encouraged states' rights and secession.

Very early in the war, a group of Charleston men feared that John C. Calhoun's buried remains would be desecrated if the city ever fell to Union troops. In order to protect the body of South Carolina's foremost proponent of states' rights, these men determined to rebury his body in a secret location. Under the cover of darkness, the coffin was disinterred from the west side of St. Philip's Church cemetery and hidden underneath the church stairwell through the following day. The next night, a second group of laborers reburied the body in the east cemetery of St. Philip's Church. Only a few men, including the African-American sextons of St. Philip's Church and the nearby Huguenot Church, knew the exact location of the reburial. Calhoun's coffin remained undisturbed in its secret location until 1871, when he was finally reinterred in his original grave.[18]

Caroline Jamison Jenkins undertook a similar mission to safeguard her father's remains. Caroline endured tremendous loss and heartache during the war. During the span of a year, she lost her two-year-old son, her mother-in-law, her father and her husband, Brigadier General Micah Jenkins. While she was still grieving the loss of her beloved husband, who had been killed by friendly fire at the Battle of the Wilderness, Sherman's troops began moving into the Palmetto State. Caroline's concern immediately shifted toward protecting her father's remains. Recently, her father, D.F. Jamison, a signer of the Ordinance of Secession, had been buried in Orangeburg. According to family history, Caroline and a servant went and moved the body to a nearby swamp to guard his body and grave from desecration by Union soldiers. After the war, Jamison was reinterred in the Orangeburg Presbyterian Cemetery.[19]

Although Calhoun's grave and Jamison's grave were not disturbed by the Union soldiers moving through the state, not all cemeteries remained unscathed. Magnolia Cemetery and other church graveyards in Charleston experienced damage from the Union bombardment of the city. However, some destruction was more deliberate. According to local history, the graveyard at Trinity Episcopal Church in Columbia suffered damage when Union troops, believing that local civilians had hidden their property there, attempted to open some of the graves and crypts. Throughout South Carolina, in places like Lancaster and Barnwell, residents still recount stories of Yankees stabling their cavalry horses in local churches and ransacking Southern cemeteries in search of buried loot.

The chaos caused by Sherman's occupation of Columbia in February of 1865 placed an enormous strain on the city's ability to care for the dead in a proper manner. William A. Nicholson, a Confederate hospital aide stationed at South Carolina College, recorded that seventeen men died at the hospital

Many of the graveyards in Charleston suffered damage from the Union bombardment of the city. *Courtesy of Library of Congress.*

during the three days of Union occupation. Expressing the overwhelming difficulty of the circumstances, he continued:

> *It was impossible to secure planks to make coffins, and it was with the greatest difficulty that I was able to get a trench dug...All I was able to do for them was to wrap their precious forms up in sheets and wherever it was possible for me to learn their names, I would mark the grave, or rather the position that they occupied in the trench, with such material as I could get in order that their friends might remove them if desired.*

During the two days that followed, Nicholson repeated the trench burials with an additional eighteen dead. One of the deceased included a widowed female hospital attendant who left behind two young children. Nicholson sorrowfully recalled, "When I realized that it would be my painful duty to consign her unconfined to the grave, I felt then the terrible horrors of the war. We laid her away in a grave by herself. If ever tears of genuine sorrow were shed, it was over the grave of this poor woman."

Between February and June of 1865, Nicholson claimed he helped to oversee the burial of at least seventy-five individuals in Columbia, not all of whom were soldiers. His only consolation remained that "as matters began to settle down, those that died, later on, were decently interred." Jane A. Doogan, who assisted in overseeing the reburials, confirmed that soldiers initially buried in trenches at the "back of South Carolina College" were reinterred at Elmwood Cemetery.[20]

When the Confederate army and government collapsed during the spring of 1865, families throughout the South experienced an intensified aching from the loss of loved ones. Families had to come to terms not only with the deaths of their loved ones, but also with the death of the Southern Cause that they had shed their blood to defend. In South Carolina, the close nature of family and friendships within a particular town or county quickly turned personal grieving into communal mourning. Communities united to decorate located Confederate grave sites and to work toward the reburial of their beloved soldiers. In the hope of finding solace in wake of the fresh bloodshed, society forged new ways to mourn and remember.

As surviving veterans and civilians attempted to find closure, they were haunted by the memories of the war and the accounts written to them by their lost loved ones. Letters written home became a tenuous link to their beloved dead. These voices from beyond the grave refreshed the memories of the living. Tally Simpson wrote such a letter of bittersweet solace to his sister, Anna, in September of 1862, one year prior to his death:

> Oh! Sister, how my heart is filled with gratitude to God for his mercy toward me and his kind protection of my life thus far…I earnestly entreat that you all will continue to pray that I may continue in the path of righteousness, and that should I fall, it shall be in defense of a glorious cause with a sweet assurance of a home in Heaven.[21]

CHAPTER 2

"CAROLINA, RECEIVE THY RETURNING CHILDREN"

Gathering the Dead and the Reconstruction Years

In accordance with my promise I saw that your beloved son's [James] remains were removed to the cemetery…I went to the spot with the man who has the removal of the bodies in charge, and with your letter in hand and the boards which were left marked, each box and number on them so there could be no possible mistake…the fourteen were taken up and buried in rotation as they were before…There was a small gold cross and locket attached to the guard…The fatal ball I also took from the same place. It was under the breast bone.
—Mary J. Dogan's letter to John S. Palmer of Lenud's Ferry, South Carolina, on June 16, 1870[22]

Through this self-assumed and unenviable task of reburying Confederate remains from the Manassas battlefield into a permanent cemetery, Mary Dogan hoped to provide comfort to Southern families who were unable to travel or reclaim loved ones lost during the war. Although they had the means to relocate their son's remains, the Palmer family determined that his final resting place should be next to his fallen comrades. Thus, the Palmers worked with Dogan to oversee that James's body was transferred to Groveton Cemetery, just outside of Manassas, Virginia. Additionally, they paid for a large, permanent headstone to mark his final resting place.[23]

James J. Palmer enlisted into Confederate service on April 13, 1861, with the Palmetto Guard of Charleston. During the reorganization of the guard, James reenlisted in the Palmetto Sharpshooters to serve with five classmates from Wofford College in Spartanburg: Thomas C. Duncan, Theodotus L. Capers, H.A. McSwain, Whetfort Smith and R.A. Watson. Disaster first struck the group when Thomas Duncan was killed in action at the Battle of Seven Pines. Horrified at the prospect of leaving his comrade's fallen and unidentified body behind on the battlefield, James pinned a note to Duncan's shirt requesting that the body be sent to his brother, Reverend James Duncan, in Richmond.[24]

The four remaining classmates continued to fight throughout Virginia with their regiment, carrying with them the memory of their fallen friend. On the last evening of the Battle of Second Manassas, not even two months after Duncan's death, the four soldiers were lying down together to rest from the fighting. Unexpectedly, a single Federal artillery shell exploded above them, instantly killing all four of the young men. One of the bullets inside the shell lodged itself in James's breast, resulting in his death. Eight years later, Dogan oversaw the removal of this fatal bullet from his breastbone and sent it to James's father.[25]

Despite the illusion of closure brought by the letter and objects, the pain of losing James was reawakened within the lives of the Palmer family. His mother, Esther Simons Palmer, lamented, "Do you know when I saw those sacred relics I could not but regret that she had not placed them with his remains. They were precious to him and ought to have gone with him. I cannot bear the idea of their passing from hand to hand after death." Holding to this belief, his mother requested that these sacred items be buried with her upon her death. In accordance with his wife's sentiments, John S. Palmer, a signer of the Ordinance of Secession, decided to be buried with a piece of James's bone fragment as well as the bullet that had delivered the fatal end to his young son's life.[26]

During the years of Reconstruction, the heavy cloud of death and mourning consumed the South, where nearly one in three men had died. It proved impossible to live when the dead remained improperly mourned and buried. In addition to working toward basic survival, Southerners felt strongly about the need to gather their dead and create suitable cemeteries in order to honor their memory. South Carolinians believed that this important task, which actually originated during the war years, should be continued regardless of the financial burden or logistical hardships. Unlike efforts for Union soldiers, no Federal or state money was provided to complete the Confederate burials and cemeteries. Lacking government funds, the people of South Carolina, especially the women, dedicated themselves to fundraising in a time of economic poverty to properly reclaim and rebury fallen Southern soldiers.

Initially, most Southerners could not reclaim and rebury the Confederate dead resting on distant battlefields. They therefore focused on those soldiers buried nearby that had not been properly cared for due to wartime constraints. Local cemeteries became a place not only to care for the dead, but also a shrine for the living to mourn Confederate soldiers when their individual loved one's remains could not be located or reclaimed. In many ways, these local graveyards served as surrogate dead for mourning lost loved ones. Accordingly, community-based memorial services became an important aspect of the South during Reconstruction.

The first Southern Memorial Day occurred in Columbus, Georgia, in 1866. Despite their limited financial resources, communal grieving helped communities refocus toward achievable commemoration activities. Mrs. Charles J. Williams explained, "We cannot raise monumental shafts and inscribe thereon their many deeds of heroism, but we can keep alive the memory of the debt we owe them by dedicating, at least one day in each year, to embellishing their humble graves." The implementation of Memorial Day services quickly spread throughout the South and later the country as a whole.[27]

In conjunction with the establishment of Confederate Memorial Day, that same year, many Ladies Memorial Association (LMA) groups started forming from wartime Ladies Aid Societies. In many instances, as with Mary Amarintha Snowden of Charleston, the president of the Soldier's Relief Association continued serving as the leader of the newly formed LMA.[28] These memorial groups organized for the purposes of establishing Confederate cemeteries or cemetery plots, planning Memorial Day services and erecting monuments. Mildred Lewis Rutherford outlined the mission of the LMA:

> *The main work of the Memorial Associations at first was to gather the dead bodies of the fallen brave from battlefields and roadsides and place them in cemeteries nearby that flowers could be placed upon their graves and orators rehearse their brave deeds. But today it is for the caring for the graves and arranging the Memorial Day exercises, uniting with the Daughters of the Confederacy in all lines of educational work and monument building.[29]*

Each LMA functioned as an independent association under the auspices of the Confederated Memorial Associations of the South. Mirroring its wartime efforts, the LMA obtained revenue for commemorative projects through subscription campaigns, hosting entertainment events and organizing bazaars.

The lack of adequate headstones in town cemeteries posed a widespread problem for LMAs throughout the state. Due to wartime constraints, most Confederate headboards were wooden planks that deteriorated over time. Subsequent weathering resulted in the soldier's identity fading from the wood and being forgotten. Mrs. Joseph Marshall of Abbeville later recalled, "Twenty soldiers died here and were buried in the Episcopal Churchyard, and at Long Cane Cemetery. After the war, Mrs. Samuel McGowan and

Mrs. J.W. Marshall got up an entertainment, the proceeds of which were used to mark each grave with a marble upright piece at head and foot."[30]

Maintaining a known soldier's identity was a paramount concern for Victorian society, especially in the wake of the war. On distant battlefields and in local hospitals, the loss of identity through wartime conditions produced immeasurable difficulty and suffering for families attempting to determine the final fate of their loved ones. Local LMAs recognized the importance of maintaining soldiers' identities in hopes of providing other families with the knowledge of a loved one's fate. Additionally, these marble headstones preserved the honor of local soldiers. The replacement of these headstones was a prolonged and expensive endeavor, lasting well into the 1900s.

Prior to the installment of the Reconstruction legislature in early 1867, the Charleston LMA contracted with the state government to obtain $1,000 as well as granite and marble. Originally intended for the State House, the stone had been damaged during Sherman's occupancy of the city. The Charleston LMA wanted to use the stone for new Confederate headstones and a monument in Magnolia Cemetery. However, before the LMA could obtain the money or the stone, the Reconstruction legislature took control and revoked the previous agreement. At the persistence of the LMA president, Mary A. Snowden, the Reconstruction legislature finally relented on the stone, which was then carved into nearly eight hundred graves. The remainder of the stone was saved and later used for a permanent monument.[31]

Although the LMA eventually received its promised stone, the conquest of the South Carolina political framework by the Republican Reconstruction legislature adversely impacted the activities of the LMA. Prior to the establishment of the Reconstruction legislature, a general time of mourning and remembrance occurred throughout the state on June 16, 1866. In Charleston, businesses closed out of respect for the Confederate dead and to allow employees to attend memorial services at Magnolia Cemetery. After the Reconstruction legislature took office in 1867, the Charleston LMA decided to curtail memorialization activities, stating "that all addresses, odes, and so forth be omitted, the graves of our noble dead to be quietly and unobtrusively decorated, so as to prevent all excuse for interference or collision with what would prove annoying." Under the shadow of this decree, Henry Timrod penned his famous 1867 Memorial Day "Ode." Although the Memorial Day events proceeded, they were scaled back from their 1866 levels in hopes that the Federal soldiers would have no excuse to interrupt the services.[32]

Nevertheless, the Federal Reconstruction troops found ways to interfere and make political statements with Confederate commemoration activities. At Elmwood Cemetery in Columbia, Reconstruction troops purposely

Confederate Monuments and Cemeteries of South Carolina

Reconstruction-era Union graves placed directly in front of the Confederate section of Elmwood Cemetery. This burial decision constantly reminded Columbians of the reestablishment of the Union within the heart of the Confederacy. *Courtesy of Kristina and Tommy Johnson.*

buried their dead directly in front of the Confederate section. During commemoration activities, Columbians would first have to walk past the dead of the Eighth U.S. Infantry in order to reach the Confederate section. They could not mourn the Southern dead without being constantly reminded of the reestablished Union presence in the state's capital.

Additionally, Reconstruction affected the shape and form of monumentation throughout South Carolina. Monuments erected during Reconstruction represented grief for the loss of human life and the Confederacy while also demonstrating an unbroken spirit of Christian hope. In the South, these monuments served as communal, surrogate headstones to remember and mourn the unclaimed dead. By establishing a local monument, families could mourn and commemorate the loss of a loved one buried hundreds of miles away. In South Carolina, all four monuments that were dedicated during Reconstruction were dedicated in privately owned areas, especially cemeteries, which reflected the mourning spirit of a community. However, the placement also reinforced the fact that these monuments could not be erected on public-owned property as long as the Reconstruction regime controlled the South Carolina government.

The town of Cheraw founded a local LMA in 1866 because, as Virginia C. Tarrh vowed, "Nor was the women's work done when the fighting was over." In the waning months of the war, the town hall in Cheraw was converted into a Confederate hospital. Soldiers who died there were taken to St. David's Episcopal Churchyard for burial. To honor the remains of sixty-two Confederate soldiers, the LMA initiated a substantial fundraising effort in order to erect a monument in the cemetery. Amazingly, within one year, it had raised $1,000 for a monument, which it contracted to local sculptor J.H. Villeneuve.[33] Proud of its accomplishments, in 1903, the Cheraw *Chronicle* boasted:

> *What a monument to woman's devotion! In a land that was neither a food-producing or manufacturing one, and through which Sherman had just marched through with his horde, leaving behind him desolation and a desert of ashes, the patriotic women of the town determined that a suitable memorial should be erected to the memory of their brave soldiers.*[34]

On July 26, 1867, the finished monument was erected in a square enclosure that held approximately fifty unmarked Confederate graves. The following day, the citizens of Cheraw dedicated the first permanent Confederate monument in the entire former Confederacy. Appropriately, the state that first seceded also became the first to dedicate a permanent tribute to its Southern soldiers.[35]

Villeneuve designed the monument as a sixteen-foot-high capped obelisk, instead of being pointed at the peak. Every angle of the design was taken into consideration when determining the inscription. The engravings did not seek to vindicate the Southern Cause; instead, the language was mournful and filled with Christian symbolism. The north face of the monument was engraved with a funerary urn and was inscribed: "TO THE MEMORY/ of/our Heroic Dead/who fell at Cheraw/during the War 1861–1865." The west side has a relief of an anchor and the inscription: "Loved and honored though unknown/HOPE." In popular Victorian cemetery culture, anchors symbolized hope in Jesus Christ and an afterlife referred to in Hebrews 6:19. On the east side, toward the direction of Christ's second coming, the monument again references the sentiments of Christian hope: "Fallen but not dead." Additionally, it includes Stonewall Jackson's famous dying words of a peaceful life after death, "Let us cross over the river, and rest in the shade of the trees." On the south side of the monument, the inscription does take a more political tone: "Stranger, bold champions/of the South revere;/ and view these tombs with love—/Brave heroes slumber here." Symbolically

Dedicated on July 26, 1867, the Cheraw monument holds the distinction of being the first permanent Confederate monument in the South. *Courtesy of Kristina and Tommy Johnson.*

Details on the Cheraw monument reflect Christian hope through Victorian funerary symbolism. *Courtesy of Kristina and Tommy Johnson.*

placed on the south side of the monument to speak to all future Southerners, this inscription reminds observers of the heroic sacrifice of brave unknown soldiers who rest beneath the monument.

One of the most interesting elements of this monument is its failure to actually use the terms "Confederacy" or "Confederate." This exclusion was highly unusual, as every other monument dedicated after the Cheraw monument mentions the Confederacy. Although phrases such as "our heroic dead" and "brave heroes" conjure images of the Confederate soldier, it does not explicitly mention the defeated nation. According to local history, the captain of a Federal garrison stationed in Cheraw prohibited the word "Confederate" on the monument. The captain wanted the monument to only honor the soldiers' ultimate sacrifice and not to glorify the Confederate Cause. Undoubtedly, this feeling was common among Union commanders. On July 18, 1866, General Benjamin Butler in New Orleans issued an order stating, "Notification is hereby given for the information of all concerned that no monument intended to commemorate the rebellion will be permitted to be erected in the borders of the Gulf."[36]

Even the dedication address for the Cheraw monument had a moderate tone when compared to those given just a few years later. Judge J.H. Hudson of Bennettsville, who had served as lieutenant colonel of the Twenty-sixth South Carolina Infantry, delivered the dedication address for the day's ceremonies. His speech detailed the significance of monumentation, beginning with the ancient Greeks at Thermopylae, and expounded on the virtues of dying for one's state. His speech did not attempt to justify the Southern Cause; he said that task would be left up to history. Instead, Hudson eulogized:

> *In mournful silence we approach this spot to erect and dedicate this simple monument to the memory…and who now sleep the sleep of death in the same grave with that of the Sunny South which they loved with more than a filial devotion…We ask not that the blood of the slain be avenged. To history we leave the vindication of their conduct…We only seek to fulfill in a humble manner our duty to the dead, and to comply with their dying wish to be remembered for their valor and steady obedience to the laws of their state.*

Hudson's speech reinforced the rightness of monumentation because such tributes offered a permanent reminder of the soldiers' sacrifice.[37]

Other than omitting all references to the Confederacy, the Cheraw monument typified the design and location of early South Carolina monuments. During Reconstruction, only four known monuments that honored soldiers from a particular county or town were erected in the Palmetto State. All of these monuments consisted of the funerary design and were located on private property, mainly cemeteries. However, it is possible that more than four monuments were erected in the state during these years, since some early monuments were made of wood, which decayed over time. For example, in 1867, Darlington County erected a white wooden shaft to the memory of the Confederacy on the lawn of the Baptist church. Once it began to decay, the LMA replaced it in 1880 with a stone obelisk in front of a local public school. A few years later, the town moved the stone obelisk to the county courthouse. There is no reason to assume that the instance in Darlington County was unique in any respect. Therefore, other South Carolina towns might have erected temporary monuments to the Confederacy that were subsequently forgotten, similar to the wooden headboards of soldiers' graves.[38]

During the later years of Reconstruction, when the economy started to rebound, Southerners organized to reclaim the battlefield dead. Circumstances of finances and proximity had hampered most desires for reburial by private families. Weighing heavily on the hearts and minds of many Southerners were the Confederate dead still resting in their shallow trench graves in Northern soil, especially at prison camps and the battlefield of Gettysburg. In 1871, the Charleston LMA determined to recover the South Carolina Confederate dead at Gettysburg for reburial within Magnolia Cemetery. The Charleston LMA contracted with Dr. Rufus Weaver, whose father, Samuel Weaver, had overseen the reburial of the Union dead in 1863. Describing the situation in 1863, Samuel Weaver had observed, "In searching for the remains of our fallen heroes, we examined more than three thousand rebel graves. They were frequently buried in trenches, and there are instances of more than one hundred and fifty in a trench."[39]

The conditions of battlefield burial had nearly eradicated all the evidence of the soldier's identity. Some farmers had watched over the burial trenches and tried to keep them in the best condition possible. Other trenches had been left unattended and were practically destroyed by time. Unfortunately, some less scrupulous farmers attempted to extract payment from the LMA before the removal of the Confederate bodies on their land.[40]

When remains were identified as being those of a South Carolinian, Weaver noted the location and reconciled his findings with earlier burial records and maps. Altogether, only eighty-four remains could be located and identified as South Carolinians. Without burial shrouds or coffins, the remains of soldiers buried in trench graves were often intermingled and unable to be separated. When reburied at Magnolia Cemetery, they were placed in a common grave. For instance, "Common Grave 24" holds the remains of seven soldiers from the Third South Carolina Infantry. Weaver identified that these men had originally been "buried West of Rose's Barn under a large Cherry Tree, the grave was deep with a board cover, all lay side by side and were undoubtedly buried by their comrades."[41]

"Common Grave 28" contains the remains of nine soldiers originally buried at the Rose Farm who were killed in battle on July 2, 1863. A large, white common marker lists their names and contains an engraving of an angel of victory crowning a fallen soldier's head. Interestingly, recent research had tied four of the men in this grave to two of Alexander Gardner's wartime photographs. Gardner's first image shows four South Carolina soldiers laying in wait for burial with a marked headboard resting on each. The men were all from Company I, Second South Carolina Infantry of Kershaw's Brigade: Private Thomas Screven Gadsden, Private Septimus Charles Miles, Lieutenant William Lowndes Daniel and Private Edward James Mills. Gardner's second image shows a fifth soldier, Sergeant Thomas Sligh of Company E, Third South Carolina Infantry of Kershaw's Brigade, in an extremely shallow trench grave. Eventually, all of these men were buried in a common trench grave alongside three Georgians. In 1871, Dr. Weaver removed nine South Carolinians from this grave and sent them to Magnolia Cemetery. Sligh (Sligth), Gadsden, Mills and Miles were reburied together in "Common Grave 28." It is unknown what happened to Daniel's remains, although without a burial shroud it is likely that his identity was intermingled with that of his comrades.[42]

On Confederate Memorial Day in 1871, South Carolinians gathered to dedicate the new graves of the Gettysburg reburials. The day began with a welcome by Lieutenant General Richard Anderson, followed by a prayer composed by Reverend John Bachman. Due to Bachman's age and health, Reverend Ellison Capers delivered the prayer. The pupils of the Confederate

The shallow battlefield trench grave of South Carolinians who were eventually reinterred in "Common Grave 28" at Magnolia Cemetery. *Courtesy of Library of Congress.*

"Common Grave 28" contains the remains of nine South Carolinians killed during the second day of fighting at the Battle of Gettysburg. *Courtesy of Kristina and Tommy Johnson.*

Widow's Home and local gentlemen then sang an ode composed by Dr. J. Dickson Bruns. Reflecting the spirit of Timrod's 1867 "Ode," the choir sang:

> *For these no sculptured shaft shall rise,*
> *Nor storied urn emblazon them;*
> *But sobbing waves and wailing skies*
> *Will sound their fitting requiem.*[43]

Afterward, Anderson introduced Reverend John Girardeau to deliver the main address for the dedication ceremony. Girardeau expounded on how these soldiers had died before experiencing the remaining battles of the war or the difficulties of Reconstruction. Reverting back to his service as a chaplain with the Twenty-third South Carolina Infantry, Girardeau recounted how soldiers in their last moments expressed a desire to be sent back to South Carolina for burial. He proposed to the crowd, "Was it that their latest moments of consciousness they recoiled from the thought that their graves would be designated as those of rebels and traitors?" He continued,

> *Afflicted Carolina, rise in thy mourning weeds, and receive thy returning children to thy maternal breast! Pillow them softly there, for there they prayed to sleep their long and dreamless sleep!…Here let them sleep with those who never looked upon a conqueror's flag floating over the citadels of a sovereign State, but closed their eyes upon a still free and defiant Commonwealth. Shoulder to shoulder they stood; now let them lie side by side. Confederates in life, confederates let them be in death.*[44]

Although the occasion was meant to mourn the dead, the treatment of the Confederates at Gettysburg combined with the problems of Reconstruction influenced Girardeau's speech to include fiery political expressions. Continuing his address with an excoriation of contemporary issues, he asked the audience if these men had indeed died in vain, or if their spirits would be vindicated by the love of liberty against despotism. He charged the crowd,

> *Our brethren will not have died in vain if we, their survivors, adhere to the great principles for which they contended unto death; if we preserve an attitude of protest against those Radical influences, which threaten to sweep away the vestige of constitutional rights and guarantees, to pollute the fountains of social life, and ultimately to whelm our civil and religious liberties in one common ruin.*[45]

Following Girardeau's address, Reverend Edward Miles read a poem that he had written for the occasion. The choir then sang "Ode Upon the Return of the Gettysburg Dead," composed by Reverend C.S. Vedder. While the mournful notes lingered in the air, the graves were filled with the sandy Carolina soil. Girardeau's words were ever present in their minds: "We are not yet done burying our dead. We are now standing by the open graves of those who died for liberty, who died for us." As the graves were closed, the ladies and children decorated the area with wreaths and floral crosses. At the center of the burial ground, where a permanent monument now stands, the LMA created a large evergreen cross interwoven with white lilies and inscribed "In Memoriam—R.E. Lee." As a reminder of Christian hope, the lilies and the evergreen symbolized the renewal of life and the promise of the resurrection.[46]

This ceremony honoring the Gettysburg dead marked the only organized large-scale reburial of Confederate South Carolinians from a battlefield into a central cemetery within the state. As the Charleston LMA explained, "Those who fell and who lay in the battlefields of Virginia and Maryland we felt reposed among friends and sympathizers, but it was not so with those who fell in Pennsylvania."[47] South Carolinians who died at other battlefields were taken to local cemeteries designated to hold the Confederate dead, as happened to James Palmer's remains. These battlefield cemeteries continue to be a vivid reminder of wartime death and sacrificial service on the Southern landscape.

Visiting the Confederate cemetery near Groveton, Virginia, that holds the remains of soldiers from the Manassas battlefields, Mrs. J.E. Alexander lamented in 1893 that the "hand of time has been busy; the fences are down; the grass has grown tall and rank over the graves of the 500 men who sleep here." Gazing across the vast field graves of those who never returned home, she observed one in particular that seemed to ease the solemn pain of the endless rows of headstones. Not knowing the soldier or the family, Alexander was comforted by the sight of James Palmer's

> white tombstone [which] *stands as a lonely sentinel over his 500 comrades who lost their lives in the first and second battles of Manassas.*[48]

CHAPTER 3

"ONE DESTINY FROM OCEAN TO OCEAN"

Beaufort National Cemetery

The idea of subjugating the South…We believe there will be no necessity for such a course…How long before the jubilant day of peace will arrive, and the rebel and the loyal soldier shake hands fraternally over the many hard-fought battle-fields, is beyond our comprehension.
—*editorial,* Port Royal New South, *November 21, 1863*[49]

On November 7, 1861, Beaufort and the Port Royal area fell into Union control. Quickly thereafter, the area transformed into a bustling nexus of Union activity along the South Carolina coast. It provided the perfect staging area and recruitment center. Furthermore, Northern abolitionist missionaries came to the area in order to help educate and promote the welfare of the newly freed slaves. The unique circumstances surrounding the town influenced the Northern missionaries' ideas of life after the war, as demonstrated by the above wartime perspective. Published in the *Port Royal New South* on November 21, 1863, the editorial reveals an intriguing and perhaps unexpected Northern desire for future peace and reconciliation among those currently engaged in armed combat.[50]

As in Columbia, Greenville and other Southern cities, Beaufort soon needed to establish a permanent burial ground for the soldiers dying in the town's hospitals and nearby battlefields. With the authorization and finance of the Federal government, Beaufort established a national cemetery to hold the remains of the Union dead. However, in a truly unprecedented wartime burial situation, Northerners in the Beaufort area decided to bury Confederate prisoners of war from nearby Hilton Head Island in their newly established national cemetery. Therefore, like other town cemeteries throughout the Palmetto State, the Union Beaufort National Cemetery created a Confederate section and still remains today as a place of Confederate memorialization.

The layout of the 7,500 graves of white Union soldiers, United States Colored Troops (USCT) and Confederate soldiers remains as a reminder of how Republican Northern nationalism and hopes of reunion unexpectedly embedded themselves in the South Carolina landscape. Beaufort provided an interesting experiment for reestablishing the Union identity in the newly seceded South. Through design principles and burial decisions, Beaufort National Cemetery represented the desires that Republican missionaries and Union officers in the town held for the outcome of the reconstructed nation and the transformed South.

Throughout the American Civil War, President Abraham Lincoln and his advisors endeavored to properly memorialize fallen Union soldiers. On July 17, 1862, Congress authorized Lincoln to purchase "cemetery grounds" to be "used as a national cemetery for the soldiers who shall die in the service of the country." The interpretation of how to create these cemeteries varied widely depending on the individual beliefs of the Union officers and civilians enacting the orders.[51]

On February 10, 1863, Lincoln issued orders authorizing Major General David Hunter and other Union officials to procure land at tax sales within the state of South Carolina for military or other specified purposes. Among other purchases, Union officials approved the acquisition of sixty-four acres of land in Beaufort for seventy-five dollars. General Hunter, General Rufus Saxton, Judge Abram D. Smith, Dr. William E. Wording and Dr. William H. Brisbane were the government agents for this purchase, and they were instrumental in planning the cemetery. The last three of these men were Northern Republican missionaries who had arrived in Beaufort in order to assist the Union army with the freedmen population.[52]

During March of 1862, the first Northern missionaries, known as Gideon's Band, arrived on the steamer *Atlantic*. Before the war ended, several hundred more Gideonites would arrive in Port Royal, hopeful for reform. One of these missionaries, William Henry Brisbane, was a native South Carolinian and outspoken abolitionist who had moved to Ohio with his slaves in order to emancipate them during the 1830s. His charismatic personality became a polarizing force in Beaufort. Together with his trusted ally, William Wording, Brisbane fought to control the distribution and use of the government-confiscated land. Their opponents were General Saxton and Judge Smith, backed by minister Mansfield French, Secretary of the Treasury Solomon P. Chase and *Free South* editor James G. Thompson. Although the debate concerning how to best divide the confiscated Confederate land was complicated and rife with scandal, both sides honestly desired the best possible outcome to promote the advancement of the freedmen and the Union agenda in the South.[53]

Confederate Monuments and Cemeteries of South Carolina

The idea of reshaping the Southern landscape in the service of a Republican Union ideal intrigued the missionaries and officers stationed in Beaufort. Lincoln's request for a national cemetery provided a perfect opportunity for the commission to establish a permanent memorial to abolitionists in the North. As one veteran bitterly stated:

> *To a considerable extent in Southern soil, and in the very presence where bold Treason reared its ungrateful head, they* [national cemeteries] *shall teach the children, whose fathers sought to dismember and destroy the Republic, to cherish it institutions, and to seek its honors and rewards.* That Nation which respects and honors its dead, shall ever be respected and honored itself.[54]

Soldiers dying for Union nationalism sanctified the Republican dream of an emancipated country, and their interment on Southern land further strengthened that ideal.

The tax commission selected the Polly's Grove tract of land for the national cemetery for several reasons. In keeping with contemporary cemetery development concepts called the rural cemetery movement, the land was far enough away from the main town for health reasons, but it was close enough to allow easy access for visitors. The placement of the national cemetery in the Polly's Grove tract as opposed to other plots outside of downtown Beaufort becomes further significant when it is understood in relation to the surrounding area, the freedmen's village of Higginsonville. Located near this community, a national cemetery filled with Union dead who helped to secure the slaves' freedom would serve as a constant reminder of the Northern blood sacrifice. This reminder would hopefully secure the permanent loyalty of the freedmen for the Union, but especially for the Republican Party, which worked tirelessly on their behalf.[55]

Prior to the interment of any soldier, the commission had to construct a burial plan for the Polly's Grove plot. The layout that it chose reflected the pastoral cemetery movement and had unique Union design characteristics. In 1855, Adolph Strauch revolutionized Victorian cemetery design by renovating Spring Grove Cemetery in Cincinnati to reflect his new "landscape lawn plan." The pastoral cemetery, or the lawn park cemetery, utilized an open landscape that relied on balance and symmetry. This design plan was more formal and less picturesque than the previous rural cemeteries. Strauch emphasized open space with fewer trees, a manicured landscape and straighter roads instead of the meandering pathways of the rural cemeteries. Symbolically, the pastoral cemetery movement continued the democratic ideals of community, family and nation by creating a cemetery that anyone could enjoy as a free public park. The developers of Beaufort National Cemetery implemented Strauch's ideas in the cemetery's arrangement.[56]

Union officials in Beaufort selected a semicircular arrangement, which was a common Union cemetery design during the Civil War. Uncomplicated pathways cut across the open vista of the semicircle, which was meant to reflect the democratic principles of the Union, especially equality. Ideally, soldiers fought for equality in life and, therefore, they should be equal in death. Soldiers were supposed to be buried without deference to rank within the army or socioeconomic conditions. Although Union officials shaped the landscape to reflect these ideas of the Union, the interments in the cemetery were often those soldiers whose remains were unidentifiable or whose families were too poor to bring them home. Nevertheless, the cemetery's physical presence sanctified the causes behind the bloodshed of the Civil War, even if the plan did not fully achieve its aspirations of democratic equality. In the semicircular arrangement, soldiers were buried in state sections. This popular Civil War burial practice reflected the state-oriented mindset of Union nationalism. An overwhelming majority of soldiers in the Civil War enlisted with a state regiment, and their national identity was firmly tied to that of their state.[57]

Regardless of soldiers' circumstances, each man was buried in an individual grave with a wooden headboard marked with the soldier's name, regiment and date of death, when known. The original headboards cost about $1.23 per board and they only lasted approximately five years before deterioration erased the very information that the headboards were supposed to preserve. In 1873, after extended squabbling in Congress, new marble headstones were finally approved for use in the national cemeteries. On April 28, 1904, Congress approved the use of the standard military grave for civilians buried in national cemeteries. After extensive debate, Congress decided to provide military headstones for Confederates buried in national cemeteries. The legislation passed on March 9, 1906, and it specified that the gravestones be pointed on top to differentiate Confederates from Union soldiers. All of these types of gravestones are represented in Beaufort National Cemetery.[58]

An immediate problem developed: what should be done with deceased USCT and Confederate soldiers? The tax commission desired a cemetery that encompassed its views of the idealized national identity, the war and the hopes for reconstruction. The abolitionist missionaries in Beaufort believed that with education and time, freedmen could become full and responsible members of the reformed Republic. Additionally, former Confederates

Beaufort National Cemetery

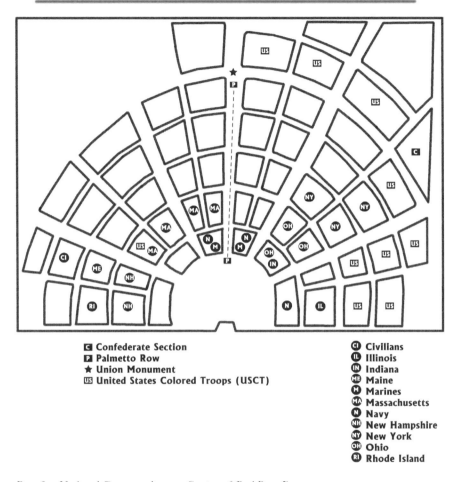

G Confederate Section
P Palmetto Row
★ Union Monument
US United States Colored Troops (USCT)

CI Civilians
IL Illinois
IN Indiana
ME Maine
M Marines
MA Massachusetts
N Navy
NH New Hampshire
NY New York
OH Ohio
RI Rhode Island

Beaufort National Cemetery layout. *Courtesy of Paul Dunn Jr.*

would need a niche within this new Union, even if that role was a minor and subjugated one. The Union army and missionaries hoped that future generations of Southerners would eventually understand the rightness of the Federals and desire full participation in the Union. Thus, Northerners had to be willing to provide the infrastructure for this reunion. This ideology became central to the burial arrangements at Beaufort National Cemetery, and it did not take long to enact this Union burial plan. Records demonstrate that workers interred USCT as well as Confederate remains in the cemetery starting in 1863, the same year that white Union burials began.[59]

Wartime burials within Beaufort National Cemetery. This image shows the wooden headboards often utilized during wartime burials. *Courtesy of New York Historical Society.*

In order to cope with the USCT wounded, the army developed a segregated USCT hospital, Beaufort Hospital #10, which opened on April 12, 1863. This hospital occupied a position of prominence after the assault on Fort Wagner, which was led by USCT troops. Following this assault, the *Free South* and the *New South* listed USCT casualties alongside those of white Union troops. Initially, the lists were segregated, but by August of 1863, the newspaper printed the name of USCT troops in the same list as white soldiers. In response to the assault on Fort Wagner, the paper reported that the USCT soldiers "seem not to be afraid to trust themselves in the field of battle, though others are inclined to doubt them, we can trust them henceforth." To the Republican missionaries, the blood sacrifice of the USCT became the proof needed to establish freedmen in the fabric of national identity. Therefore, their placement in the national cemetery was not only proper, but it was necessary in order to prove the freedmen's worth in the Union.[60]

Wartime USCT burial sections are spread throughout the semicircle in places of prominence and are mainly organized as U.S. Regular Army troops instead of state soldiers. The only state section of USCT burials is an integrated section of white and black Massachusetts burials. The other USCT burials are located on the left side of the cemetery. Although they may initially appear outside of the semicircle, they are actually located next to white Union sections. Furthermore, the placement of the USCT sections mirrors white state burials on the opposite side of the cemetery. The USCT soldiers are not relegated to a back section or a separate cemetery; instead, they are placed within the Union national identity.

The United States Colored Troops (USCT) section contains the remains of freed South Carolina slaves who served in segregated Union regiments during the war. *Courtesy of Kristina and Tommy Johnson.*

All unidentifiable Union soldiers were placed in unknown graves toward the back of the cemetery, regardless of race. A fitting example of this situation is the Fifty-fourth Massachusetts Infantry burials, highlighted in the movie *Glory*. After the assault on Fort Wagner failed, Confederates unceremoniously threw USCT Colonel Robert Shaw's body into the mass grave of African-American soldiers. During the war, Shaw's body was never recovered, and he remained buried in the trench with his men. Sometime between 1865 and 1868, the Union bodies recovered from Morris Island (Fort Wagner) were reinterred in Beaufort National Cemetery as unknowns. Although Shaw's burial with his USCT troops was a purposeful degradation, other accidental intermingling of USCT and white Union remains must have occurred. Oftentimes, battlefield necessity of burying men as quickly as possible in shallow trench graves precluded any societal notions of proper burial practices. Thus, when a trench was opened after the war, the remains of USCT soldiers and their white counterparts often became indistinguishable during the reburial identification process.[61]

The same chaos of battlefield interments often caused the intermingling or misidentification of Confederate soldiers as Union soldiers. It is therefore extremely likely that misidentified Confederates lay interred as Union soldiers throughout Beaufort National Cemetery. There are 114 known Confederate graves in the national cemetery that were interred during the war: 3 Alabamians, 8 South Carolinians, 11 Floridians, 5 Tennesseans, 22 Georgians, 13 Virginians, 3 Kentuckians, 13 North Carolinians and 36 additional Confederate soldiers. These men are buried in the back right corner of the cemetery. In 1997, the Sons of Confederate Veterans dedicated a monument in honor of all of the Confederates buried in the cemetery.[62]

The Confederates buried in Beaufort National Cemetery were prisoners who either received medical treatment in Beaufort or were held in a prisoner of war camp on Hilton Head Island, such as South Carolinian Robert S. Stowe of Pickens. Stowe enlisted at age thirty-five in Company K, First South Carolina Cavalry (also known as Company D, First South Carolina State Cavalry Battalion), and was initially taken prisoner at Upperville, Virginia, in July of 1863. Paroled a few days later at City Point, he reenlisted with the Confederate army. He would not be as fortunate the second time he was captured. On December 13, 1864, Stowe was taken prisoner at Pocotaligo, South Carolina, where he had been severely injured in the fighting. He was taken to the prisoner of war camp at Hilton Head Island, where he died eighteen days later from his injuries. Stowe's remains were sent to the Beaufort National Cemetery for interment.

The practice of interring Confederates in a national cemetery rarely occurred and it was definitely not part of the original Congressional framework authorizing these cemeteries. The act stated that the grounds purchased would be "used as a national cemetery for the soldiers who shall die in the service of the country." Although the legislation did not specify that only Union burials would transpire in the government-purchased land, its implied meaning was evident. Furthermore, wartime cemeteries such as Gettysburg, Arlington and Antietam purposely excluded Confederates from reburial into their national cemeteries. What then led to this broad interpretation of "service of the country"? These facts demonstrate significant ideological motivations for burying the Confederate dead in Beaufort National Cemetery. There was no obvious reason why they would not simply be buried in a local private cemetery, as was done in most Union-controlled areas. Furthermore, it made little practical sense to transfer the Confederate dead prisoners from Hilton Head Island to Beaufort.[63]

There could be several plausible explanations for including Confederates in the national cemetery. Although a staunch Unionist and emancipationist, Brisbane, a native South Carolinian, likely believed that many of these young Confederate boys were simply pawns of the powerful planter class. Perhaps sympathy toward these men, although believing their cause completely wrong

One of eight South Carolinians buried in the Confederate section, Robert S. Stowe from Pickens enlisted in Company K, First South Carolina Cavalry. Wounded and captured in the fighting at Pocotaligo, he died a few days later at Hilton Head Island. *Courtesy of Kristina and Tommy Johnson.*

and immoral, led to some greater understanding that even the Confederates deserved a proper burial.[64]

Possibly more powerful, however, was the recognition that although the Northerners could reform the South and reshape its landscape, the defeated Confederates would someday have a role in the reconstructed Union. Many of the Northerners in Port Royal believed that a generation or two would pass before the South could fully participate in the Union, but they were encouraged that, with time, healing would eventually occur. As early as April of 1863, the *New South* printed speeches and editorials by Republicans advocating a position of future reconciliation. In his address to Congress, Republican Speaker of the House Galusha A. Grow of Pennsylvania insisted, "Whether the night of our adversity is to be long or short, there can be no doubt of the final dawn of a glorious day…there can be but one nationality… The traditions of the past and the hopes of the future have crystallized in the American heart the fixed resolve of one Union, one country, and one destiny from ocean to ocean." Grow's remarks encompassed the hope of reunion and one nationalistic identity forged throughout the entire country. However, he recognized that for this to happen the South must not only be defeated, but it also must be properly rejoined with the nation.[65]

When the war finally concluded in April of 1865, the nation shifted its resources from fighting to reburying the dead in permanent cemeteries and formulating Reconstruction policies. Major General Robert Ogden Tyler was placed in charge of the Quartermaster's Department in Port Royal in order to oversee the reburials of soldiers' remains from trenches and graves throughout the area into Beaufort National Cemetery. On March 12, 1868, he reported on the state of cemetery: "The work of removing bodies from the state of S.C. to this Cemetery will be completed during the present month, removals from Georgia and Florida which are contemplated will not be finished untill [*sic*] the 1ˢᵗ of May." Tyler further mentioned that internal improvements were currently under construction, such as the superintendent's residence, walkways and the avenue network. The work for these additional projects was most likely completed by the USCT.[66]

Despite best efforts, not all of the Union bodies were removed to Beaufort National Cemetery. This problem was especially true in instances when reburial records were either lost or never created. For instance, little evidence exists concerning the fate of any Union soldiers buried in Columbia during the war—either those who died at the prisoner of war camp or those who died during the fire of February 17, 1865. It is widely believed that these soldiers were reburied in Beaufort National Cemetery, but as of yet no direct evidence has surfaced. The only known Union remains left in Elmwood Cemetery are those

During the war, 257 Union soldiers were buried at the Charleston Race Course, as shown in this image. Of these burials, 154 soldiers were reinterred in Beaufort National Cemetery. *Courtesy of Library of Congress.*

of the troops stationed in the town during Reconstruction. In Aiken, the Union dead from the cavalry fight were buried in the First Baptist Aiken graveyard, where part of the fighting occurred. These dead were not removed and still remain in a tidy row of twenty Union gravestones outside of the fellowship hall. Interestingly, they share the same burial space as the Confederate dead from the battle. Unfortunately, a 1911 memorial to an unknown Confederate cavalryman who died at the battle has since fallen over and is in disrepair.

In 1868, Beaufort National Cemetery underwent boundary changes due to confusion over the wartime tax sale. In a contract with town officials on April 10, the federal government agreed to lease the national cemetery lands for a period of ninety-nine years and allow the town oversight powers to assure that the federal government would properly maintain the cemetery grounds. Additionally, the federal government permanently relinquished control of thirty-six acres of land to the City of Beaufort for a municipal cemetery. This land was renamed Evergreen Cemetery and is located across present-day Boundary Street. During the early years of this agreement, "Evergreen Cemetery" became the common name for the entire municipal and national cemetery area. This unique arrangement demonstrated the close association that the town officials established with the federal government in relation to the national cemetery.[67]

The United States government decided to commission disabled Federal soldiers as superintendents "to watch over and protect the graves, and wait upon visitors" of the seventy-six national cemeteries created during and immediately after the war. In 1870, Captain Niels Christensen was appointed superintendent of Beaufort National Cemetery. Christensen was born in Denmark on January 31, 1840, and he immigrated to the United States in 1862. Upon his arrival, Christensen joined a New York regiment and was wounded twice during the war. Christensen's interest in agriculture made him a perfect candidate for completing the work at Beaufort National Cemetery.[68]

Influenced by Strauch's pastoral cemetery movement, Christensen wanted Beaufort National Cemetery to have a park-like appearance while still maintaining a sense of decorum and nationalism. He enlisted the help of prominent Beaufort citizens and garden clubs in order to achieve his landscape design. Through the fundraising efforts and private donations of several ladies of the town, Christensen purchased the materials necessary to landscape the cemetery. The Port Royal Agricultural School, a freedmen school operated by the Christensens, donated money to purchase plants for the cemetery and possibly helped to plant many of the trees and shrubs.[69]

Present-day landscaping in Beaufort National Cemetery reflects Christensen's plans. In keeping with the principles of the pastoral cemetery movement, Christensen maintained an open vista and did not clutter the landscape with excessive horticulture. Many of the trees in the cemetery today, such as the oak and the magnolia trees, are most likely those purchased by Christensen.[70]

Perhaps the most prominent feature of Christensen's landscape design is the palmetto tree row, which frames the center avenue of the cemetery. Drawing influence from the South Carolina landscape, the palmetto-lined avenue utilizes the same design principle as the live oak– or magnolia-lined entrance to a grand Southern plantation home. Christensen symbolically selected the palmetto tree for this entrance since it is the emblem of the state of South Carolina. Christensen intended for this palmetto-lined avenue to reflect the principles of the Union. The use of the palmetto symbol as a reestablishment of the Northern presence in South Carolina was not unique to Christensen. Both the *New South* and the *Beaufort Republican* newspapers utilized the palmetto tree as part of their trademarks. Christensen's powerful use of this symbol in the national cemetery strengthened the idea of the evolving South.[71]

A Union monument donated by Mrs. L.T. "Eliza" Potter, a Northerner who resided in South Carolina during the war, stands at the end of the palmetto row. The imposing granite obelisk is inscribed, "Immortality to hundreds of the defenders of American liberty against the Great Rebellion."

The impressive Palmetto Row reinforced the Union presence in the state with a prominent South Carolina symbol. *Courtesy of Kristina and Tommy Johnson.*

The dedication of the monument occurred sometime between the cemetery inspection report on May 17, 1870, and before Decoration Day activities in 1879, when Laura Towne, a Northern missionary, mentioned it in a letter to her sister. Towne wrote, "I like the inscription on the monument very much… It is out of fashion nowadays to use such plain words, but there they stand, in granite." These remarks reveal that the monument must have been dedicated some years prior. More significantly, Towne believed that the presence of such a monument would permanently remind visitors of the causes of the Civil War and the rightness of the Union. Towne's remarks demonstrate how the monument's strong sentiments had become increasingly unpopular in Beaufort and instead were replaced by a spirit of reconciliation.[72]

Due to personality conflicts, the adjutant general's office relieved Christensen from his post as superintendent of Beaufort National Cemetery in 1876. Outraged, forty-eight Beaufort citizens, including Union missionaries, African Americans and former Confederates, signed a petition of support for Christensen that detailed the extensive work that he had accomplished for the cemetery. Although the petition failed, the variety of signatures demonstrates how much had changed within the town of Beaufort since the conclusion of the war. Since the cemetery reflected the interests of each of these groups, the various factions in town united

The Union Monument at Beaufort National Cemetery (unknown dedication date). *Courtesy of Kristina and Tommy Johnson.*

in order to provide the best possible care for their national cemetery and their dead.[73]

During the postwar years, the cemetery functioned as a gathering place for the residents of Beaufort to memorialize the soldiers and the causes of the Civil War. Even though they gathered in the same space, the memorial activities of the Southerners and Unionists have mostly been separate despite reconciliatory rhetoric. Union Decoration Day, now known as Memorial Day, has been continuously celebrated in Beaufort National Cemetery by both blacks and whites; however, it has evolved over time.

Although Decoration Day activities in the national cemetery were mainly reserved for Unionists, the newspapers and memorial speeches reflected conciliatory overtones. In 1873, the *Beaufort Republican* printed a conciliatory poem: "Nor ask our hearts who wore the blue/Nor who the faded gray/Since battle's sweat crimson dew/All hate hath washed away." A few weeks later, the *Beaufort Republican* published a "Roll of Honor" naming all of the Port

Royal natives who lost their lives in service of the Confederacy. The list was compiled by Dr. J.A. Johnson, who also signed the petition to keep Christensen as superintendent of the national cemetery. Johnson serves as a prominent example of someone who fought to reclaim their place within the Union while remembering their Confederate past. In the national cemetery, he could respect the Union dead while still mourning his own loss. It is doubtful that Johnson or any other former Confederate would have possessed such strong sentiments about the cemetery had there been no Confederate interments.[74]

In 1877, the *Beaufort Tribune* and *Port Royal Commercial* explained that "it was impossible to place flowers on every grave, so the ladies made about thirty handsome wreaths, one for each State represented and one each for the soldiers of the regular army and the sailors." Although the newspaper failed to explain if the ladies honored the USCT dead as part of the regular army, African Americans participated in the formal Decoration Day activities.[75]

As white interest declined in celebrating the Republican Union viewpoint of the war, African-American support for Decoration Day activities remained strong and became a political outlet for contemporary politics. In 1879, approximately ten to twelve thousand African Americans from across South Carolina and Georgia gathered at Beaufort National Cemetery to honor the Union army and the sacrifice of the USCT soldiers. Laura Towne attended this memorial service with freedmen students from the Penn School. Although they again laid wreaths for each of the states, Towne lamented the lack of white citizens attending the ceremonies.[76]

During the 1890 Decoration Day activities, African Americans congregated to listen to speeches about contemporary race relations. During the day, they held a parade to the cemetery and placed American flags on all of the soldiers' graves. Six years later, the tradition of using Decoration Day as a political platform continued with Reverend William Palmer's address. Palmer taught classics, English and literature at the State Colored College in Orangeburg, South Carolina. In his oration, Palmer attempted to recommend solutions to the national problem of racial segregation. He offered the example of the Union army as a rallying point for blacks and white Northerners: "Black and white fought upon the same battlefield; they rallied around the same flag; they were wounded by the same enemy; they died for the same cause; they were buried in the same cemetery; their souls took flight to the same God." He proceeded to insist that reconciliation between the North and the South would help African Americans. Once again, Beaufort National Cemetery served as a platform for dealing with the problems of racism and sectionalism.[77]

Presently, on every Memorial Day, the federal government places a small American flag on every grave in the cemetery, including the Confederate graves. Thus, the 7,500 Civil War soldiers interred in Beaufort National Cemetery have transcended the label of "Yankee," "Rebel" or "Colored" to become honored American soldiers.

Each Confederate Memorial Day, celebrated on May 10, members of the local General Stephen Elliott Chapter of the United Daughters of the Confederacy (UDC) place small Confederate battle flags on the Confederate graves within Beaufort National Cemetery. When questioned how long this tradition has been occurring, a UDC representative stated that the commemoration has happened "for as long as anyone can remember." Prior to the UDC chapter forming in 1910, the Confederate graves were probably memorialized by individuals as well as the Ladies Memorial Association. Community memorial services and the placement of small battle flags on the Confederate graves continue to the present day.[78]

Burial arrangements and landscape design demonstrate the importance of Beaufort National Cemetery as a monument to the unique circumstances of the South Carolina Sea Islands during the war. The design of Beaufort National Cemetery assisted white Northerners, freedmen and former Confederates in finding a role within the new fabric of Beaufort society and the developing postwar national identity. On Port Royal Island, Northerners recognized an opportunity to reform the freedmen population without interference from hostile Southerners. African Americans were instilled with a new sense of pride about their status as freedmen. They educated themselves in politics and joined the Union army in order to promote their own freedom. Once the war concluded and former Confederates returned to the drastically changed Beaufort landscape, they also began to develop a place in the newly established society.

In order to live and work together in peace, these three groups had to discover commonalities to create a basis for communication. The common ground of the national cemetery established a space in which mourning for one's own dead could occur near one's enemies. This is not to imply that racial peace or harmony between Northerners and Southerners completely existed within Beaufort. However, the cemetery provided the space for a greatly needed commonality in the postwar years. Within the landscape of Beaufort National Cemetery, what had the possibility of becoming a divisive reminder of the Union occupation remains as a permanent symbol of the idealized New South. Ultimately, all factions could agree,

All that a grateful country can do, is by honoring the memories, and protecting the sacred remains of those who laid down their lives for its salvation, to show its appreciation of the heroic sacrifice, and teach to succeeding generations lessons of undying patriotism.[79]

CHAPTER 4

"A GRAND MANIFESTATION OF HONOR"

Vindicating the Southern Soldier and Cause

The occasion was designed as a grand manifestation of honor to the dead Confederate soldiers and reverence of their memory, and of appreciation of the work of the women who have perpetuated those feelings in a tangible and viable form.
—*Charleston* News and Courier, *May 14, 1879*[80]

Filled with vivid descriptions and editorial commentary, the Charleston *News and Courier* printed a large feature article of the events on May 13, 1879. That day, a crowd of approximately fifteen thousand citizens and veteran soldiers from across South Carolina gathered at the State House grounds in Columbia to celebrate the unveiling of the South Carolina Monument. The long-anticipated memorial became the first monument dedicated on public property in the state. Its unveiling inaugurated a new era of memorialization in the Palmetto State aimed at vindicating the Confederate soldier, especially in prominent public spaces.[81]

Although mourning had been a public and communal event in the immediate postwar years, the politics of Reconstruction had constrained monuments in their location and sentiment. With the end of Reconstruction in 1876, more South Carolina towns felt comfortable and were finally allowed to erect monuments in the public sphere without fear of reprisal. Popular locations included courthouse lawns, public parks and in the middle of streets. Unlike activities held on private property, these places necessitated government approval. The passage of time and the proper reburial of most Confederates had lessened the overall urgent need to mourn. These factors, combined with the easing of hardships and the return of political power, allowed Southerners to embark upon a mission dedicated to the political and social vindication of the Southern Cause. Former Confederates wanted to prove to the North that although the South had suffered military defeat, the Lost Cause for which they fought was noble and the South was once again a political force. These changes also meant that a new ideology would play an active role in monument inscriptions. The language of active mourning was replaced by a resolute idea of vindicating the Southern soldier and Cause. In the North, a similar pattern of glorifying the Union and disparaging the South also began to form. Monuments served as an outlet to express anger and resentment. Additionally, they attempted to teach future generations the Southern or Northern version of events.[82]

In November of 1869, while the state was still under Reconstruction, the ladies-only South Carolina Monument Association (SCMA) initiated a plan to create a monument for all South Carolinians who had died during the war. Originally, SCMA proposed to place the monument on private property at Arsenal Hill overlooking Sydney Park. The State House lawn was not considered due to "the state being under Radical rule." A geological survey, however, revealed that a layer of quicksand at the Arsenal Hill location could not hold the weight of the monument. The committee decided to move the monument to Elmwood Cemetery and entered into a contract with the Muldoon, Walton and Cobb Company of Louisville, Kentucky, to erect the monument on August 1, 1873. At some point between 1873 and 1875, a granite base was placed in the cemetery.[83]

The main portion of the monument was purchased from Italy and wrought by the famed sculptor Nicoli. When the monument arrived from Italy in 1875, however, the committee did not have the funds to pay the remaining $10,000 balance. The Italian company agreed to let the monument remain in South Carolina until SCMA raised enough funds to pay the outstanding balance. In 1876, SCMA's fortunes drastically improved when Wade Hampton was elected governor and the native Democrats regained control of the legislature. Two years later, the legislature unanimously approved a measure that allowed the monument to be built on the State House grounds. Furthermore, the state legislature contributed funds toward the outstanding balance, while individual legislators contributed private donations.[84]

Outside of any government assistance, according to an undated ledger, SCMA had raised at least $11,084.40 from local counties, bazaars and politicians. Legislators had given no less than $40.00 in private funds. The LMA raised $1,407.30 at two bazaars that it organized. At the inaugural ball for Wade Hampton, attendees gave $97.11 toward the monument. The two counties with the highest donations were Richland at $2,296.05 and Charleston at $1,494.45. Some counties struggled to give more than others, such as Pickens County, which only gave $5.00, and Hampton and Marion Counties, which only gave $10.00 each. Wisely, SCMA had invested the money from the onset of fundraising and gained $76.93 in interest toward

South Carolina Monument Association.

APPEAL.

Women of South Carolina, there needs no urgent appeal to your sympathies in a cause so sacred as that which we now undertake. The great tide of adversity which has swept over our unhappy land, has hitherto stifled effort in this direction; but not, therefore, have our hearts ceased to beat for the glorious dead. Scarcely is there one among us whose thought does not, on the first mention of our object, turn at once, with loving affection, to some grave which this monument is intended to honor.

Mothers, widows, sisters, daughters, whose hearts thus cling to the soldier's grave, let us then unite with an earnest, loving effort in this holy duty. Let even our lisping little ones be brought to give their mite to its accomplishment; that thus impressed upon their minds, they may never forget to love and honor the memory of those who battled and fell in our cause. If a lost cause, even therefore the more holy. Even therefore does it become the more incumbent upon us, to bring to this great sacrifice of pure purpose and heroic deed, that homage and veneration which the world pays only to success.

With the wish that all who have shared in a common sorrow, may share also in the privilege of raising this testimonial to our lost heroes, the annual subscription for membership is put at the lowest point practicable; that thus it may be within the reach of those, who, having little to give, have still the right, through tears and suffering, to join us in the fulfilment of this most sacred duty.

To all others—men as well as women, old and young—to all who cherish the name of Carolinian, and cling with a fond love to whatever is left to us of our "good old State," we would say, give to us freely according to your means; give generously; give gratefully to the memory of those who gave their lives for us.

A Reconstruction-era fundraising appeal from the South Carolina Monument Association. *Courtesy of South Carolina Confederate Relic Room and Military Museum.*

the monument. With inflation and the expenses involved with relocating the base of the monument two times, the project exceeded the original $10,000.00 budget.[85]

The 1879 monument dedication turned into a weekend-long event, revolving around Confederate Memorial Day. Moreover, the events symbolized a celebration of the end of Reconstruction. Just a few years prior, it would have seemed impossible that former Confederates would gather in such a large number, freely speaking their minds, and dedicate a monument to the Confederacy on the State House grounds. The excitement of such an occasion practically eclipsed the mournful sadness of dedicating the monument to the Palmetto State's fallen soldiers in gray.

Generals Wade Hampton and M.C. Butler were originally scheduled to attend the monument dedication. Political business, however, kept the pair in Washington. In their stead, Governor W.D. Simpson and General M.L. Bonham served as the presiding officer and chief marshal, respectively. The ladies of SCMA, along with several prominent men in the town, provided meals for the veterans and active state militia. Veterans carried flags from their former units, which were used to decorate the speakers' stand. These flags included Washington Light Infantry, Hart's Battery, First South Carolina Volunteer Infantry, Palmetto Sharpshooters, Second South Carolina Volunteer Infantry, Palmetto Guard Volunteers, Seventh South Carolina Volunteer Infantry, Lafayette Artillery, Twenty-fourth Volunteer Infantry, Orr's Rifles, Richmond Volunteer Rifle Company of Columbia, Irish Volunteers of Charleston and German Volunteers. The unit flags served as a reminder of the soldiers' wartime sacrifices.[86]

The completed monument was dedicated at the northeast corner of the State House, located at the current public entrance to the building. Unfortunately, the monument's location proved problematic, but not for political or social reasons. Instead, the spot proved to be a lightning rod during heavy thunderstorms and the monument was struck numerous times. The final lightning strike occurred on June 22, 1882, just three years after the monument's original dedication. The force of the bolt knocked the soldier from atop the monument, leaving only its feet on the shaft. The extent of the damage forced SCMA to replace the soldier and move the monument to its present location at the intersection of Richardson (Main) and Gervais Streets. On April 23, 1884, SCMA rededicated the monument at its new location. The rededication was a smaller event that included a simple tribute of flowers and an artillery salute by the Columbia Flying Guards. The stone soldier on top of the monument, originally made in the image of Brigadier General Stephen Elliott, had to be replaced. Referring to the new monument soldier, Colonel J.C. Hemphill explained, "The new monument is fully as handsome as the first but differed in several details. The soldier's hat has a broader rim, the canteen is different, the soldier's face is almost unchanged." However, Mrs. A.T. Dargan, the only surviving member of the original SCMA, disagreed: "In point of manly strength and beauty, the new face and figure are not equal to the original."[87]

The placement of the monument reinforced its power as a symbol of Southern resistance. Its closeness to the State House resulted in a continual and unapologetic reminder of Southern resurgence. Moreover, the monument was topped with a soldier who stood on picket duty, actively on guard and facing northward. His presence reminded Southerners that the Northern threat still lingered, while also warning the North that the South would still fight for its rights.[88]

The South Carolina Monument provides an excellent example of how South Carolinians attempted to cope with the legacy of the war while making

The old face of the South Carolina Monument prior to being struck by lightning and relocated to its current location. *Courtesy of South Carolina Confederate Relic Room and Military Museum.*

The South Carolina Monument, dedicated 1879. *Courtesy of South Carolina Confederate Relic Room and Military Museum.*

their voices permanently heard in the immediate wake of Reconstruction. One of the primary concerns among Southerners was how future generations would remember the Confederate generation. For example, when explaining its reasons for holding the first statewide conference, the Confederate Survivors' Association of Charleston District asserted in 1869:

Confederate Monuments and Cemeteries of South Carolina

The State House complex, circa 1909. *Courtesy of Library of Congress.*

We owe it to ourselves, to the gallant Dead, to the truth of History, to Posterity, to the Women of the land, and, above all, to that Humanity of which we are a part, and which is always ennobled by the contemplation of Freedom and of earnest and heroic effort, that the truthful incidents of that mighty struggle for Honor and Constitutional Right shall live forever.[89]

Southerners feared that the Yankee interpretation of the war and its causes would infect future generations. The importance of family and community within Southern culture made this looming shadow of Northern interpretation even more dreaded. Thus, many Southerners pursued varied means in order to impart their side of the story in permanent manifestations. Southerners definitely did not attempt to conceal their reasons for creating these permanent historical interpretations etched in stone and bronze on the Southern landscape. The president of the Southern Memorial Association of Fayetteville, Arkansas, unabashedly declared:

These monuments we build will speak their message to unborn generations. These voiceless marbles in their majesty will stand as vindicators of the Confederate soldier. They will list from these brave men the opprobrium of rebel, and stand them in the line of patriots. This is not alone a labor of love, it is a work of duty as well. We are correcting history.[90]

Freed from the constraints of Reconstruction and with the immediacy of mourning fading, the education of future generations was elevated to a level of importance that rivaled, if not surpassed, remembrance of the dead through erecting monuments.

The correction of historical interpretation for future generations was a critical reason that SCMA engaged in erecting the South Carolina

Confederate veterans gathered in front of the South Carolina Monument during a reunion held in Columbia, circa 1905. *Courtesy of South Carolina Confederate Relic Room and Military Museum.*

Monument. The message was further enhanced by its unique and prominent location on the State House grounds. Speaking to Southerners, this mission of correcting history was inscribed on the south side of the South Carolina Monument:

> *Let the stranger/Who may in future times/Read this inscription/Recognize these were men…/Whom defeat could not dishonor…/And that from her* [South Carolina] *broken fortunes…/Teaching all who may claim/The same birthright*

Additionally, SCMA's post-dedication report expressed that the two main reasons for the monument were to "perpetuate the memory of the slain and convey to the latest generations the record of the undying fidelity of the people of South Carolina."[91]

As the message on the south face of the monument addressed the sons and daughters of the Palmetto State, the north face of the monument lectured those above the Mason-Dixon Line, proclaiming:

> *This monument/Perpetuates the memory,/Of those who…/Died in the performance of their duty/Who have glorified a fallen cause,/By the simple manhood of their lives,/The patient endurance of suffering/And the heroism of death,/And who/In the dark hours of imprisonment,/In the hopelessness of the hospital,/In the short, sharp agony of the field,/Found support and consolation/In the belief/That at home they would not be forgotten.*

Although seemingly solemn, the message reminds the North that although the South had suffered military defeat and horrific events during the war, the sacrifice of the boys in gray would be forever remembered at home. Furthermore, the monument implies that the North has responsibility for the Confederate deaths, especially those that occurred during imprisonment.

Following the example of the South Carolina Monument, defiant soldiers and language remained a common element of many Palmetto State monuments in the era of post-Reconstruction and Southern vindication. From 1878 through 1903, of the eighteen monuments dedicated to groups of soldiers from a geographical area (not regimental), half contained soldier-topped monuments. Of these soldier-topped monuments, 67 percent were in active or defiant poses. Only three monuments during these years contained a soldier in a passive stance. The remaining nine monuments were designed in the funerary motif of an obelisk. Furthermore, only four were placed in

The active duty soldier atop the Orangeburg District Monument (1893) has a highly detailed uniform and expression. *Courtesy of Kristina and Tommy Johnson.*

Not all of the monuments dedicated immediately following Reconstruction contained militaristic soldiers. Some monuments still maintained funerary aspects. The Newberry Confederate Monument, dedicated in 1880, combined funerary and military elements by capping the obelisk with cannonballs. *Courtesy of South Carolina Confederate Relic Room and Military Museum.*

cemeteries; the other fourteen were located on public property. Although the style of these monuments reflected the ideas of mourning and not active fighting, their public location and often defiant language marked a distinctive shift away from the somber graveyard monument of the Reconstruction years. The message instead reflected an overt political statement of resurgence.

With the end of Reconstruction, the possibility of erecting monuments in the public domain meant a general shift away from placement in cemeteries. Altogether, in South Carolina between 1878 and 1993, only seventeen of the sixty-one monuments dedicated to soldiers from a particular geographical region were originally placed in cemeteries. A staggering 72 percent of county monuments dedicated after Reconstruction were originally placed in public

Dedicated in 1900, the towering thirty-two-foot-tall obelisk in Edgefield contains minimal inscriptions. General M.C. Butler praised the design in his dedication address: "Its simplicity and durability illustrate the rugged unaffected courage and valor of Edgefield's Confederate soldiers." *Courtesy of Kristina and Tommy Johnson.*

locations. The monumentation patterns from this time period symbolize the general desire of South Carolina memorial committees to shift from privately owned property to prominent locations in the public sphere.

One notable monument dedicated in a cemetery during this time period was the Defenders of Charleston Monument in the center of the Confederate section of Magnolia Cemetery. Although dedicated in a cemetery, the Defenders of Charleston Monument was not a typical funerary monument. As discussed in the previous chapters, Magnolia Cemetery and the Charleston LMA served as the premier Palmetto State memorial organization. The effective women's leadership, the prime location of Magnolia Cemetery and the city's affluence helped this LMA achieve remarkable accomplishments.

Twelve years after the base of the monument was dedicated, the LMA unveiled the full monument in an elaborate memorial ceremony on clear and crisp Thanksgiving Day, November 30, 1882. The granite comprising the base of the monument was the stone that was originally promised to the Charleston LMA but had been delayed by the Reconstruction legislature. Appropriately, the granite of the monument's base was hewn from the same donation of damaged State House stone used to create the eight hundred marble headstones buried in the Confederate section of Magnolia Cemetery.[92]

Major H.E. Young, chairman of the gentlemen's auxiliary to the Charleston LMA, opened the ceremonies at 2:00 p.m. after a parade of veterans and associated civilians entered the cemetery. He introduced Major Theodore G. Barker as the presiding officer for the occasion. Barker gave a few remarks and then Reverend John Girardeau opened the official proceedings in prayer.[93]

Upon the closing of the prayer and a solemn song, the guns of the German Artillery fired a thirteen-gun salute. The salute prompted the unveiling committee to step forward. The committee consisted of "Miss Ethel Dawson and Miss Julia Courtenay, wearing dresses representing the Confederate States flag; Miss Harriet Kershaw and Miss Maggie O'Hear, wearing dresses representing the flag of the State of South Carolina; Miss T. Williams, Miss Pearl Tabor, Miss Lottie Olney, and Miss Lela Davis, wearing white dresses with blue sashes." The young ladies were assisted by Captain F.W. Dawson, Major Louis G. Young, Colonel James Armstrong, Captain Virgil C. Dibble and Captain W.D. Palmer. At the last salute, the young ladies pulled the cord, sweeping aside the South Carolina state flag that concealed the monument. As the monument was revealed, the flag was hoisted up onto the nearby flagpole. The audience erupted into applause at the dramatic unveiling.[94]

After the unveiling, Barker introduced the two main speakers of the day, General M.C. Butler and General B.H. Rutledge. Reverend W.H. Campbell

Confederate Memorial Day at Magnolia Cemetery, circa 1910. *Courtesy of Library of Congress.*

then read an ode written by Miss E.B. Cheeseborough. The closing refrain rang out:

Be woman's task to throw the light
Upon the Southland's pages;
To hold the lamp of Truth aloft,
That all the future ages
Can read the Southern soldier clear

Next, Reverend W.S. Bowman read Henry Timrod's famous "Ode to Magnolia Cemetery." The ceremony concluded with a prayer by Right Reverend Bishop P.F. Stevens.[95]

The monument consists of a square pedestal topped by an active soldier, clutching a flag against his breast and carrying a drawn sword in his left hand. This Confederate soldier was entirely un-Reconstructed. His belligerent stance continued the fight as he clutched the flag to protect it from the Federal troops, meanwhile protecting the reputation and the Lost Cause of those buried around him. Charlestonians at the monument's unveiling were impressed by the lifelike nature of the soldier, prompting a four-year-old boy to comment, "I am so glad that they didn't bury that Confederate soldier, so I could see him to-day."[96]

While some monuments resounded with new vindictive sentiments, other monuments echoed the task of generations past. The work of marking graves and creating common places of burial had not yet concluded. The same year that Charleston unveiled its monument, Florence dedicated a more solemn cemetery monument. The Florence monument served more as a common grave marker for Confederate soldiers than a typical memorial. In many ways, this monument reflected the issues surrounding the dedication of the Cheraw monument. During the war, sixty-four Confederate soldiers from various Southern states had been buried at the Presbyterian church in Florence. Since there were not individual headstones, the Florence LMA decided to erect a suitable monument over the common grave. During the spring of 1882, the organization dedicated a simple funerary obelisk, which was purchased from R.D. White in Charleston for $272. The ceremonies involved Confederate veterans, the Florence Rifles, local dignitaries, schoolchildren, citizens and the Florence and Timmonsville brass bands. Unfortunately, about twenty years later, the church property, including the graveyard, was sold to the Atlantic Coast Line Railroad Company. Since many of the original LMA members had passed away, those ladies remaining joined with the local United Daughters of the Confederacy chapter to supervise the reburial of the Confederates and the relocation of the monument. Helping to find a solution, the Mount Hope Cemetery Association graciously donated a lot to the committee. In January of 1905, the ladies directed the transfer of the Confederate soldiers and monument to Mount Hope.[97]

At the turn of the century, changes in technology and society took their toll on other monuments, resulting in their alteration and relocation. In 1892, the County and City of Greenville dedicated a Confederate monument that would become the center of a groundbreaking legal battle. Initially, the monument was erected in the middle of North Main Street in downtown

Originally placed within the Florence Presbyterian Church graveyard in 1882, the monument and the graves of sixty-four Confederates were moved to Mount Hope Cemetery in 1905. *Courtesy of Tommy Johnson.*

Greenville. The monument design was unique for the time period because it had a soldier on top at parade rest, not in the active stand of fighting or guarding. The soldier was modeled after James Blackman Ligon, the first man to enlist in the Saluda Volunteers, Company G, Fourth South Carolina Volunteer Infantry.[98]

In addition to the parade rest soldier, the inscription on the monument was not overly hostile, but rather contained elements of mourning and continued peace. One inscription reads:

> *Come from the four winds, O Breath/And breathe upon these slain/That they may live./Resting at last, in that glorious/Land, where the white flag/Of peace is never furled.*

The first half of the quotation is from a Bible verse, Ezekiel 37:9. This verse was also utilized on other Confederate monuments, most notably that of the Savannah Confederate Monument. It serves to remind onlookers of God's ability to create life after death. While the first half

Monuments continued to be erected in cemeteries for many years following Reconstruction. In 1914, residents of Summerville relocated scattered wartime Confederate burials into a single site at St. Paul's Episcopal Church. The C. Irvine Walker Chapter of the UDC dedicated this funerary monument in 1915 atop the common grave. *Courtesy of Kristina Johnson.*

The Greenville Confederate Monument as it stands today at the entrance of Springwood Cemetery. *Courtesy of Kristina and Tommy Johnson.*

of the inscription promises future resurrection, the later half praises the current peace on earth. The monument promotes the hope of continuing the "white flag of peace" between the North and the South. The language and style of the monument greatly differs from the monuments dedicated in the years immediately following Reconstruction. Overall, the monument foreshadowed the reconciliatory monuments that would become more popular in South Carolina after 1903.

Notwithstanding the more reunionist overtones, the Greenville Confederate Monument still exemplifies common characteristics of other monuments dedicated during the same time period in South Carolina. For instance, it stood at a prominent position in the community and contained similar language characteristics, such as the restoration of the Confederate soldiers' reputation:

> *Success is not the test/The world shall yet decide/In truth's clear, far off light/That the soldiers/Who wore the Gray and died/With Lee—Were in the right!*

The inscription reminds readers that regardless of the promise of continued peace, the South and the Confederate soldiers were right in their Cause. Therefore, their deaths were not in vain and future Southerners should not be ashamed of their sacrifices.

Nevertheless, the Greenville LMA could not have foreseen the changes that future technologies would produce, especially the impact of the automobile. Located in the center of North Main Street, the monument was considered a major traffic hazard. In 1922, the Greenville City Council voted to relocate the monument to the local county courthouse. The decision infuriated the local United Confederate Veterans, UDC and LMA, which did not feel that they had been appropriately consulted in the decision. Under the cover of darkness on the morning of October 11, 1922, city workers removed the soldier from the top of the monument, placed it to the side of the road and began deconstructing the base. When the workers left for lunch, concerned citizens quickly took the unguarded soldier that had been on top of the monument and placed it at an undisclosed location. Meanwhile, four local veterans secured a temporary injunction halting the monument's relocation, and court battles rapidly ensued.[99]

Rumors surfaced that the soldier was hidden on a farm on Paris Mountain Road. Therefore, it was immediately relocated to the Echols Street Fire Department. Finally, on June 9, 1924, the South Carolina Supreme Court ruled to relocate the monument. It believed that the safety of travelers was a paramount concern. Additionally, as perhaps a conciliatory token to the Confederate faction, the court asserted that quietness and peace were needed in order to fully respect the Confederate monument. Instead of relocating it to the county courthouse, a small park was constructed by moving the

Originally placed in the middle of North Main Street, the soldier on top of the pedestal was temporarily removed in 1922 by Confederate veterans protesting the city's efforts to relocate the monument. Two years later, the monument was relocated to its present location. *Courtesy of Greenville Historical Society.*

boundary wall of Springwood Cemetery. Although the monument was technically still located on public property, it assumed a more funerary role in its new location. The monument can be seen from the wartime unknown burial section and is close to the final resting place of James Ligon.[100]

As evidenced by the Greenville monument, times were changing in the Palmetto State. The South Carolina Supreme Court's decision created a flurry of relocating Confederate monuments out of city streets and busy intersections and into nearby cemeteries, memorial parks and courthouse lawns. Furthermore, the generation that had survived the war and had withstood the difficulties of Reconstruction was now joining its comrades in eternal slumber in the same cemeteries where they had honored their memory for decades. During the ensuring years, the children and grandchildren not only commemorated those who died during the war, they also memorialized those who had survived and since passed away.

Veterans in front of the Columbia Confederate Soldier's Home. *Courtesy of South Carolina Confederate Relic Room and Military Museum.*

As the sun began to set upon the Confederate veterans, Reverend John Kershaw proudly affirmed the accomplishments of the LMA and Confederate survivors. At the 1893 Confederate Memorial Day in Magnolia Cemetery, Kershaw eulogized,

> *All over our Southern country, soon were gathered groups like this, and monumental shafts, commemorative of their valor and devotion, shot up, white and glistening amidst the dark green of surrounding foliage, mute but eloquent witnesses to the silent sleepers beneath, that their deeds were not forgotten, nor their virtues buried in oblivion…And year by year richer grows the harvest…until now many more perhaps have passed over to the majority than are left to answer the roll call…Survivors, soldiers, friends, let us drop a tear to their memory, and salute their gallant and knightly spirits.[101]*

CHAPTER 5

"PARADE REST?"

Changing Monuments in Changing Societies

Parade rest! What in the world did our fellows know of parade rest? In the four years they never had time to rest, and none of us can remember being on parade. If you want a good, live Confederate, get him in action.
—anonymous, Confederate Veteran, 1908[102]

In the years after Reconstruction, outside of funerary memorials, most monuments imparted a message of vindication through defiant soldiers, defiant language or northward positioning. Choices in how to memorialize Confederate soldiers, however, drastically changed after the turn of the century. These changes imparted new meanings and messages that reflected contemporary events.

The shift from using active, defiant soldiers on top of Confederate monuments to passive, parade rest soldiers was not without contention. The anonymous author of this 1908 letter to the *Confederate Veteran* could not reconcile this shift from the realities of soldiery to the contemporary impulses behind monumentation. Monumentation, as the letter writer seemed to recognize, had become a telling tribute to reconciliation rather than the true experiences and emotions of the Confederate soldiers.[103]

New events in American society combined with a new generation of South Carolinians establishing the monuments were major factors involved in the memorialization changes. Before the turn of the century, the Ladies Memorial Association had spearheaded Confederate memorialization efforts. These women had lived through the depravations of the war, mourned their loved ones and struggled during Reconstruction. All of these experiences influenced the manner in which they chose to memorialize. Additionally, the veterans themselves played active auxiliary roles in conjunction with the LMA's activities by serving as orators at monument dedications. Their speeches often reflected the funerary aspects of the

Approximately one thousand schoolchildren formed the Third National Confederate flag on the State House steps for the 1915 Confederate veterans' reunion. *Courtesy of South Carolina Confederate Relic Room and Military Museum.*

memorials, while attempting to vindicate the Lost Cause and Confederate soldiers.[104]

With the passage of time, however, the original founders of the LMA realized that the memorialization work had not been completed and that these responsibilities needed to be passed on to a new generation. Alice A. Gaillard Palmer of the Confederated Memorial Associations of the South, the national alliance of local LMAs, explained, "As our ranks are thinned we bring in some 'daughter' or 'granddaughter,' thereby hoping to preserve our identity as an Association, and to keep up the honored custom and sacred duty of repairing once a year to lay garlands on the graves of the martyrs of the Southern Cause."[105]

During this transition, an organization with a similar mission, the United Daughters of the Confederacy, emerged in 1894. In the subsequent years, UDC chapters were formed in the same towns where LMA groups had been present. Although some ladies of the LMA believed that memorialization remained their primary responsibility, over time the two groups eventually merged as the UDC became the more prominent social organization. In Columbia, Mrs. W.K. Bachman suggested merging the Richland County Memorial Association with the Wade Hampton UDC for the RCMA's fiftieth anniversary in 1915. Sadly, Mrs. Bachman died before this union occurred.[106]

The active duty soldier standing on top of the Marion County Confederate Monument (1903) was described by *The State* newspaper as "holding his gun in a way which threatens anyone who approaches as an enemy." This soldier provides a stark contrast to parade rest soldiers. *Courtesy of South Carolina Confederate Relic Room and Military Museum.*

In South Carolina, this power transfer from the LMA to the UDC produced an almost immediate shift in the types of monuments created. In 1903, Marion County designed and erected a belligerent monument that depicted a soldier facing north with a drawn rifle. That same year, Greenwood County dedicated a passive, non-funerary Confederate monument at parade rest, which after this point would become the standard in the state. Interestingly, both of these monuments were joint projects between the local UDC and LMA organizations. In both cases, the LMA initiated the commemoration project. However, in the actively fighting Marion County soldier monument, the LMA remained the active driving force behind the project. The local UDC established a committee that worked with the LMA in the effort. In the passive Greenwood County monument, the LMA began the project but then merged into the local UDC. Therefore, over the course of the five-year project, the UDC assumed control over the final result.[107]

Although some UDC ladies, especially the older members, argued about the dangers of reconciliation, many of the younger generation were influenced by national events that demonstrated an overall trend toward reunion. Some Confederate and Union veterans also expressed interest in reunification. During the 1890s, a series of Blue and Gray Reunions promoted healing and reconciliation among the Confederate and Union veterans. Not until the Spanish-American War (1898), however, did the rhetoric of sectionalism drastically decline throughout the country. General Henry V. Boynton explained the impact of the Spanish-American War while speaking at the South Carolina Chickamauga monument unveiling in 1901: "A foreign war, [in] whose heat the last vestiges of sectionalism were consumed, and Southern and Northern veterans of the civil war and their sons by the hundreds and thousands grasped the flag of the reunited nation and carried it round the earth together."[108] The collection of these events forged a new patriotism focused on the United States as a whole, rather than the more regional identities previously held by many Southerners and Northerners. South Carolina's city and county Confederate monuments constructed during this time therefore demonstrated these reconciliatory feelings and aided in propagating this new nationalism.[109]

An interesting event combining the Spanish-American War and the establishment of the Confederate burial sections occurred at Elmwood Cemetery in Columbia. On June 27, 1898, U.S. Army Private Argyle Gilbert died suddenly in Columbia from heart disease. A native of Virginia, it proved difficult to communicate with his family concerning their wishes for his remains. The Confederate veterans of the city believed that the soldier deserved a proper burial and donated a plot to have Argyle's remains interred in Camp Hampton's Bivouac. The Camp Hampton's Bivouac section of Elmwood Cemetery, purchased by the local United Confederate Veterans camp, served as postwar burial ground for veterans. At sunrise on June 28, Confederate veterans and Argyle's fellow United States soldiers gathered to bury the young soldier dressed in his blue United States Army uniform beside those who wore the gray.

Following through on the reconciliatory promises initiated during the Spanish-American War years, President Theodore Roosevelt's

Confederate Monuments and Cemeteries of South Carolina

The local United Confederate Veterans camp purchased this section, known as Camp Hampton's Bivouac, for postwar interments at Elmwood Cemetery. *Courtesy of Tommy Johnson.*

administration implemented policies to promote national reconciliation and reunion. Roosevelt issued an executive order in 1905 to return the captured Confederate battle flags back to their original states. President Cleveland had attempted the same measure in 1887 but had to backtrack due to intense pressure from the Union veterans' group, the Grand Army of the Republic (GAR). A year later, Roosevelt appointed South Carolinian and Confederate veteran William Elliott to serve as a United States commissioner to mark the graves of the Confederate dead buried in approximately sixty-one former Northern prison camps. Forty years after the close of the war, the federal government finally became involved with the reburial and grave marking of the Confederate dead. This same task had been performed for the Union dead during and immediately after the war, resulting in the formation of national cemeteries. At the rate of $2.50 per headstone, Elliott contracted with the Blue Ridge Marble Company in Georgia to mark the graves with Southern stone. He continued his efforts until his death in 1907.[110]

With the passage of time since the end of Reconstruction and the urgent need to vindicate the Southern soldier, South Carolinians began to reconcile the concept of being a Southerner with that of being an American. Aggressive Confederate soldiers and defiant inscriptions did not readily agree with this new attitude. Between 1904 and 1922, only two of the twenty-five monuments dedicated included defiant soldiers. Ten monuments contained soldiers at parade rest.

Completed in 1911, Spartanburg Confederate Monument was one of the last active soldier monuments constructed in South Carolina. It represents a sharp contrast to the parade rest soldiers. The base of the monument is a State House column damaged by Sherman's troops. *Courtesy of South Carolina Confederate Relic Room and Military Museum.*

CONFEDERATE MONUMENT, LANCASTER, S. C.

Although the Lancaster County Confederate Monument (1909) still contained language to vindicate the Confederacy, the soldier was no longer in the active stance of fighting. Inside the monument's cornerstone, citizens placed a copy of the Ordinance of Secession, Lancaster District company muster rolls, Confederate flags, Confederate currency, letters, badges, photographs, newspapers and other assorted relics. *Courtesy of Lindsay Pettus.*

The Laurens County Confederate Monument, dedicated in 1910. Both the parade rest monument and the inscription reflect the reunionist monuments common during the time period. Furthermore, the stone for the monument base was composed of Winnsboro granite, while the soldier was carved from Vermont marble. *Courtesy of South Carolina Confederate Relic Room and Military Museum.*

The Marlboro County Confederate Monument (1907) at Bennettsville is topped with a parade rest soldier. Although the inscription contains language to defend the Confederate soldier, it also affirms reconciliation by stating, "Let us turn to the grace of forgiving." *Courtesy of South Carolina Confederate Relic Room and Military Museum.*

On August 23, 1906, Abbeville dedicated a Confederate monument that reflected mixed messages of reunion and justifying the Southern Cause. One inscription reads, "Brave men may die—right has no death; Truth shall never pass away." *Courtesy of South Carolina Confederate Relic Room and Military Museum.*

The Clinton Confederate Monument, dedicated in 1911, bears the more passive language common throughout South Carolina after 1903. *Courtesy of Paul and Paula Dunn.*

Confederate Monuments and Cemeteries of South Carolina

An interesting anecdote during this period transpired at Kingstree when the Williamsburg County UDC decided to erect a monument for their local heroes. Although the official unveiling ceremony occurred on May 10, 1910, the marble soldier did not arrive from Italy until thirty days later. Immediately, townspeople realized that something was amiss upon closer inspection of the federal design of the uniform—their soldier was a Yankee! Allegedly, local Confederate veterans went on a drinking and shooting binge to express their outrage. The UDC and the townspeople ultimately decided to place the Union soldier on top of their Confederate monument. Perhaps locals were comforted by the complacent stance of the infantryman, who stood with his kepi in one hand and rifle at rest in the other. It is highly doubtful that this lone Yankee would have been accepted a decade before; but sentiments were changing in the South and in the nation. Four years later, a Confederate soldier was incorrectly shipped to York, Maine. Like Kingstree, York decided to keep and proudly display its enemy soldier. Despite the similarity of these two occurrences, it is unlikely that the two soldiers were switched due to the four years of separation and different places of manufacturing. The real Confederate Kingstree soldier still remains missing in action, if in fact he was ever correctly produced. In 1958, the South Carolina Highway Department and the Kingstree City Council attempted to move the monument off the city street. A bitter controversy erupted. Even though the soldier was a Yankee, local citizens felt possessive of the poor displaced fellow and fought to keep him from being dismantled. Finally, the city council allowed the monument to be relocated to the county courthouse lawn. Nevertheless, when it was moved, the town changed one important aspect—the soldier now faces north.[111]

A notable decrease in the number of monuments erected in South Carolina occurred after 1915. With the onset of World War I, the Palmetto State's attention shifted away from establishing Confederate war memorials to the immediate problem of supporting the current war effort. This change of focus impacted the UDC and remaining LMAs.

In 1918, Mary Poppenheim, of the Charleston LMA and the national president general of the UDC, urged the Confederated Southern Memorial Association to extend its reach beyond its traditional duties. She declared that the organization needed to modify its constitution "to enable us not only to continue the loving memorial work for which we were organized, but also to enlarge the scope and purpose of our work to answer the calls of the present crisis." The UDC had already organized to support the current war efforts and instructed each chapter to carefully report their labor to the State War Relief director.[112]

The Kingstree Confederate Monument (1910) provides an interesting example of reunion and reconciliation. After its dedication, the townspeople realized that the form on top was actually that of a Yankee soldier. *Courtesy of Kristina and Tommy Johnson.*

Detail of the Kingstree Monument, revealing the Union characteristics. *Courtesy of Kristina and Tommy Johnson.*

Furthermore, women involved in Confederate memory on the local level organized to support the South Carolina doughboys and their compatriots. In 1917, several of the older women involved in the Richland County LMA and UDCs formed the "Girls of the Sixties," a division of the National League for Women's Service. Only women who had lived through the Confederate War were permitted to join the "Girls of the Sixties." One of their main missions was to teach the younger ladies of Columbia the proper way to patriotically support the troops. After the war ended, the "Girls" remained active as a civic club. They raised $200 for the World War Memorial fund, which was to be dedicated in honor of the South Carolinians who died during the Great War. They also donated funds toward national Confederate monument projects, such as the enlargement of the Lee Memorial Chapel at Lexington, Stone Mountain Memorial Fund and a monument at Trevilian Station. In an interesting turn of events, the Columbia Chapter of the UDC dedicated a memorial tablet in the State House in 1929 to commemorate the activities of the "Girls of the Sixties." The following year, the organization was disbanded after the death of its founder, Malvina Gist Waring.[113]

Yet again, changes in society influenced the way in which South Carolinians memorialized their Confederate heroes. The horrors of World War I made it more difficult to romanticize war through passive soldiers. As millions of soldiers died on European battlefields, the Palmetto State faced the grim reality of not just leaving its fallen soldiers on Northern battlefields, but rather on an entirely different continent altogether. These young men had been killed in horrific fashion and wasted away without burial in the middle of "No Man's Land." These feelings were reflected in the popular art and architecture of the day, resulting in the modernist movement typified by Picasso's famous *Guernica* (1937) painting of the Spanish Civil War. Current trends in art and architecture influenced memorialization in South Carolina, resulting in a third major monumentation shift.[114]

In 1922, the last two soldier-topped monuments of South Carolina were dedicated in Rock Hill and Gaffney (Cherokee County Monument). Since 1923, 99 percent of the monuments dedicated within the state were composed of either a slab or structure design. The term "slab" is used to describe monuments of engraved rectangular stones, rectangular stones with bronze tablets, rocks with bronze tablets or simply bronze tablets. Influenced by modern architecture, these monuments did not have a distinctive artistic design or intrinsic message. Harkening back to ancient Egypt, obelisks had been an obvious symbol of mourning. Fighting soldiers and passive soldiers also contained explicit messages of aggression and pacifism respectively. The design of the modern slab monuments fails to readily impart a particular

YORK COUNTY'S
CONFEDERATE MONUMENT
UNVEILING
FRIDAY, JUNE 7TH

The Monument Erected Under the Auspices of the

WINNIE DAVIS CHAPTER, U. D. C.

TO THE MEMORY OF THE HEROIC CONFEDERATE SOLDIERS OF YORK COUNTY WILL BE UNVEILED FRIDAY, JUNE 7TH.

Governor MARTIN F. ANSEL

Will be Our Gracious and Honored Guest on This Occasion and that Beloved and Superb Gentleman and Soldier

Colonel ASBURY COWARD

Will be the Orator of the Day. Take a Day off and pay your tribute of homage to the Confederate Soldiers of York County, than whom no Better or Braver ever faced the cannon's mouth.

GRAND MILITARY DAY

The 2nd Battalion, N. G. S. C., Maj. W. B. Moore and Staff, Commanding, comprising Co. "G," Cornwell (Chester Co.), Capt. J. S. McKeown; Co. "H," Rock Hill, Capt. H. S. Diehl; Co. "K," Fort Mill, Capt. T. B. Spratt, and Co. "L," Yorkville, Capt. J. R. Dickson, will line up for Dress Parade at the old K. M. M. A. School building at 11 o'clock a. m., to be reviewed by His Excellency, the Governor of South Carolina; Col. Wardlaw of his Staff; Col. A. Coward, Col. W. W. Lewis and Col. J. R. Lindsay, Maj. M. J. Walker, Capt. M. C. Willis, and Capt. J. J. Keller of his Staff.

THE LINE OF MARCH

Will form at the intersection of Congress and West Liberty Streets at 12 o'clock, noon, in following order:

1st.—Band; 2d—Marshals, mounted, J. C. Wilborn, Chief; 3rd—Militia, Maj. W. B. Moore, Com.; 4th—Confederate Veterans, Capt. W. B. Smith, Commanding; Capt. John D. McConnell, Acting Adjutant; Private R. N. McElwee, Acting Quartermaster. 5th—Carriages with Speakers and Distinguished Guests. 6th—Winnie Davis and Visiting Chapters, U. D. C. 7th—School Children from all parts of York County. 8th—Woodmen of the World, Other Organizations and Citizens. [Arriving at Monument Park the Militia will stack arms.]

A broadside for the 1907 unveiling of the York County Confederate Monument. Although the veterans wanted the monument erected at the county courthouse, the local Winnie Davis Chapter of the UDC selected Rose Hill Cemetery instead. *Courtesy of South Carolina Confederate Relic Room and Military Museum.*

The Memorial Arch to the Confederate Section at Elmwood Cemetery provides a good example of the functionality of monuments dedicated after 1923. The wrought-iron arch was dedicated in 1951. *Courtesy of South Carolina Confederate Relic Room and Military Museum.*

message. Additionally, they were easier and cheaper to produce. Moreover, the slab design lacks an overt message.

Common memorial structures were cemetery entrances, water fountains, benches and gazebos. Sometimes these elements were combined into the same monument. Along with slabs, structures continue to be the most common type of monument erected. Structures require the observer to take an active role and interact with the monument. Thus, the fulfillment of these monuments is not met simply at its dedication; the function of this design requires continued public interaction and reflection in order to obtain its potential.

A distinctive monument combining both the structural element and the legacy of the Great War is located in Calhoun County. In 1909, the Olin M. Danzler Chapter of the St. Matthews UDC determined to erect a suitable Confederate monument. Although Calhoun County had been carved out

This fountain monument (1924) in St. Matthews memorializes the men from Calhoun County who served in the Confederate army and the American army during World War I. *Courtesy of Kristina and Tommy Johnson.*

of Orangeburg County in 1908, the local UDC still wanted to recognize the Confederates from within the new county. Additionally, it wanted to honor the local soldiers who served in World War I. The joint monument was dedicated in memory of Confederate soldiers, "Our Heroes" and the "World's War Heroes." Furthermore, the ladies of the UDC selected a unique design of a four-pillar, square pediment centralized around a public water fountain. The name of the monument at its time of dedication, "Memorial Drinking Fountain," reflects its practical function at the time of its dedication in 1924.[115]

In many aspects, the Calhoun County monument serves as a natural transition into modern memorialization. Today, Confederate monuments are joined on county courthouse lawns with monuments for other wars. These more recent monuments help Southerners today to assert their modern American identity while continuing to honor their ancestors' concept of the American nation and states' rights. Even alongside modern monuments, the Confederate monument remains one of the most prominent and romanticized features of the South Carolina landscape. As Francis Horry Ticknor poetically exclaimed:

> *Knightliest of the knightly race, that since the days of old, have kept the lamp of chivalry, a light in the hearts of gold.*[116]

CHAPTER 6

"GOODNIGHT, BRAVE SOLDIER"

Unique Monuments and Gravestones in South Carolina

'Til earth and sea shall be no more,/Let marble and brass their deeds enshrine,/The laurel and cypress their memory entwine./Our heart and tongue cease not to tell,/Of those who live and those who fell.
—*Fort Mill Ladies Memorial Association, 1904*[117]

The previous chapters have predominantly explored monuments for geographical groups of soldiers from South Carolina or wartime dead buried together in cemeteries. In addition to these monuments, South Carolina also has a rich tradition of erecting memorials honoring soldiers from specific units or ethnicities, high-profile individuals, church congregations, women and even slaves. Although these monuments are more specialized in their scope, they were still constructed to impart meaning concerning the events of the war and its legacy.

Certain veterans groups desired to create lasting tributes to their unit's wartime record, especially in Charleston, where these veterans had a remarkable amount of money and influence. The German community erected a monument in 1889 to honor the local German Confederate troops in Bethany Cemetery, adjacent to Magnolia Cemetery. In adjoining St. Lawrence Catholic Cemetery, the local Irish community erected an obelisk bearing Irish symbolism. This thirty-six-foot-high granite obelisk topped by a cross cost approximately $15,000 and was dedicated sometime prior to 1894. The monument commemorates the service of the Irish volunteers in the War of 1812, Florida War and Confederate War. The Washington Light Infantry also dedicated a monument to its unit in 1891 but placed it in a downtown Charleston park.

Throughout the state, church congregations also established monuments to those from their congregation who served in the Confederate army. Most churches dedicated a tablet with the soldiers' names on their church wall.

The Confederate German Artillery Monument at Bethany Cemetery in Charleston was dedicated in 1889 with elaborate fanfare. The active duty soldier atop the monument gazes across the field of battle in anticipation. *Courtesy of Kristina and Tommy Johnson.*

A commemorative ribbon for the German Artillery Monument unveiling.
Courtesy of South Carolina Confederate Relic Room and Military Museum.

Detail from the Irish Volunteers' Monument at St. Lawrence Catholic Cemetery in Charleston (circa 1890). The obelisk contains two bronze tablets filled with symbols of Irish tradition, military service and South Carolina palmetto trees. *Courtesy of Kristina and Tommy Johnson.*

State House pillars, damaged by Sherman's troops, were requisitioned for use as Confederate monuments in Spartanburg and Greenwood and a third for use by the Daughters of the American Revolution (DAR). The current monument in the First Presbyterian Church of Columbia graveyard originally served as a monument to South Carolina's Revolutionary War generals, which was located on the State House grounds. Several years later, the DAR sold the pillar to the church for use as a Confederate monument. Dedicated in 1922, the column contains a copper tablet that lists all of the Confederate soldiers from the congregation, with a star next to the names of those who died.

The town of Fort Mill contains one of the most unique Confederate memorial grounds in the country. In the years following the war, the white population of the town descended into the economic depression that swept through the South during Reconstruction. Hoping to alleviate their sufferings, Captain Samuel Elliott White established the Fort Mill Manufacturing Company, the forerunner of Springs Industries, Inc., in 1887. The stable employment opportunities helped Fort Mill to flourish in a time when many communities were suffering. Furthermore, it provided the town with the financial resources necessary to create one of the most unique Confederate monumentation efforts in the South.[118]

Assuming the name of the former Confederate president, the Jefferson Davis Memorial Association (JDMA) was founded in 1889 by White in hopes of commemorating the local Confederate soldiers and the Lost Cause. Uniquely, men and women both composed the JDMA. Not until several years later did the association split into separate United Confederate Veterans (UCV), LMA, UDC and Sons of Confederate Veterans (SCV) organizations. Bankrolled by White's generous donations, the Jefferson Davis Memorial Association was able to erect four substantial monuments in the town's Confederate Memorial Park over the course of nine years. These monuments included honors for local Confederate soldiers, supportive women of the war, loyal slaves and the local Catawba Indian tribe.[119]

In December of 1891, the JDMA dedicated the first monument in honor of the "Defenders of State Sovereignty." Subscriptions collected by the JDMA and a large donation by White provided for the soldier-topped monument. In a unique endeavor, the monument listed all 171 Confederate soldiers, both living and dead, who served from the Fort Mill community. At the elaborate dedication ceremony, six maimed Confederate veterans unveiled the monument. Upon White's death in 1911, his funeral parade passed by the black-draped soldiers' monument on the way to his final resting place in Unity Cemetery.

The Confederate Monument at First Presbyterian Church of Columbia. Dedicated in 1922, the column contains a copper tablet that lists all of the Confederate soldiers from the congregation. A star was placed next to the names of those who died during the war. *Courtesy of Kristina Johnson.*

The Confederate Soldiers' Monument at Fort Mill (1891). A popular line from the Augustus Julian Requier poem "Ashes of Glory" was inscribed on the north face of the monument: "The warrior's banner takes flight to greet the warrior's soul." *Courtesy of Kristina and Tommy Johnson.*

The positive reaction to this first monument encouraged White to continue erecting Confederate monuments at Confederate Memorial Park. On May 21, 1895, Fort Mill unveiled two monuments—one to the women of the Confederacy and the other to loyal slaves. Both monuments are credited as being the first monuments of their kind within the Confederacy. Such memorialization reflected the idealism of the Lost Cause, which romanticized Southern women and slaves, a concept later capitalized on by Margaret Mitchell's *Gone with the Wind.*[120]

Similar to the soldiers' monument, the pedestal base is topped with the sculpture of a kneeling woman praying over a fallen Southern flag. Poetically idealizing the Southern woman, the inscription reads:

> *To the women of/The Confederacy,/the living and the dead,/who midst the gloom of war/were heroines in the strife/to perpetuate their noble/*

sacrifices on the altar of/our common country. Let/sweet incense forever/ rise, till it reach them/"in robes of victory/beyond the skies."

On the opposite side of the memorial, the inscription continues, "Many are the hearts that are weary to-night,/Wishing for the war to cease;/Many are the hearts praying for the right/To see the Dawn of Peace." The monument lacks the egalitarian nature of the Fort Mill soldier monument, as one side lists eighteen last names of mostly wealthier and influential Fort Mill women. Not to exclude others, however, the list concludes with "and with many others."

The unique monument to faithful slaves is a simple obelisk with a relief engraving on two sides. One image depicts a mammy tending to children, while the other shows an enslaved field hand gathering crops. Exalting the virtues of a "faithful slave," the monument inscription states:

The Confederate Women's Monument at Fort Mill (1895). *Courtesy of Kristina and Tommy Johnson.*

Dedicated to/The faithful Slaves/who, loyal to a sacred trust,/Toiled for the support/of the Army with matchless/Devotion, and with sterling/Fidelity guarded our defenseless/Homes, women, and children during/the struggle for the principles/of our "Confederate States of America."

The other side of the faithful slave monument lists the name of ten slaves, mostly belonging to the White family, whom S.E. White believed to appropriately fit this description. Such a message of happy, loyal slaves helped to vindicate the Confederate Cause by mitigating the evils of slavery while also implying that the races were not naturally antagonistic. Furthermore, it made it easier for future generations to defend their Confederate ancestors and the institution of slavery. Describing the monument to the Confederated Memorial Association, the local LMA asserted:

The monument at Fort Mill dedicated in honor of loyal slaves (1895). *Courtesy of Kristina and Tommy Johnson.*

It is added to the fame of Captain Samuel E. White as a builder, that he is first to crystallize into enduring marble, the Southerners' debt of gratitude to those faithful slaves who, in keeping the trust lain upon them to guard the homes, the property and honor of their masters who were serving the South on the field—will ever deserve forbearance from the people of the South.[121]

In 1900, White, along with James McKee Spratt, financed the final monument in Confederate Memorial Park. This unique monument, honoring the local Catawba Indians, contains a Catawba brave crouching behind a broken stump in the act of drawing his bow. Unfortunately, the monument has since been damaged and left unrepaired. In the cornerstone, the tribe placed a list of all the Indians on the reservation, arrowheads, arrow points, pots, jars and Confederate relics. The inscription discussed the history of the tribe while also mentioning the service of seventeen tribesmen in the Confederate army and listing their names.[122]

The Fort Mill monuments serve as an important extension of prior Confederate memorialization patterns. At a time when the South felt under assault from Northern ideas of slavery and the causes of the war, White and the JDMA determined it necessary to extend the lesson of Southern history beyond the traditional Confederate soldier to include these distinct groups. Before any discussions of American multiculturalism, the Fort Mill monuments recognized the efforts of different categories of local citizens and imposed political meanings on their wartime efforts. Ultimately, these monumentation efforts attempted to engage them in an idealized common narrative, whether or not that common narrative was historically accurate or politically correct in modern terms. Moreover, the unique monuments assisted in establishing new forms of commemoration. Through the monuments placed by White and the JDMA, South Carolinians began to honor groups outside of the traditional Confederate soldier.

The Fort Mill women's monument inspired a similar tribute at the South Carolina State House. At the statewide UCV reunion in 1897, Reverend S.P.H. Elwell argued that the actions of South Carolina women during and immediately after the war were heroic in their own right and deserved commemoration. Elwell was commissioned to oversee the project, but his subsequent death placed the entire mission at risk of being left unfinished. Finally, in 1909, the project gained momentum when Major J.G. Richards Jr. introduced an appropriation from the state legislature for $7,500 to establish the monument. These funds would only be available if they were matched by private donations. The fundraising call was more than matched. Overall, private donations and interest gained on the deposit totaled $21,000. The

The Catawba Indian Nation Monument erected within the Confederate Park at Fort Mill (1900). *Courtesy of Kristina and Tommy Johnson.*

South Carolina Confederate Women's Monument was finally completed and dedicated in 1912 at the State House grounds.[123]

F. Wellington Ruckstuhl of St. Louis, who also sculpted the Wade Hampton III monument located at the State House, designed the monument. Ruckstuhl's design incorporated an elaborate sculpture atop a pedestal-style base. The sculpture includes a woman sitting on a chair with a Bible upon her lap. Unlike the Fort Mill Women's Monument that listed mainly upper-class women, the State House monument was designed to reflect a middle-class woman at the conclusion of the war. As Ruckstuhl described the scenario, the winged figure of Genius "holds over her a crown of immortality while in her left hand she holds a palm of glory and a trumpet to announce to the world her great virtue and deeds." On one side of the woman, an enthusiastic winged boy offers the woman a tribute of unbound roses. On the other side, his winged sister timidly offers a well-organized and bound bouquet of flowers and a scroll legitimizing the monument by order of the General Assembly.[124]

No Holier Spot of Ground

William E. Gonzales, editor of *The State* newspaper, wrote the inscription for the monument. The inscription elaborated on the importance of South Carolina's Confederate women:

> *In this monument/Generations unborn shall hear the voice/Of a grateful people/Testifying to the sublime devotion/Of the women of South Carolina/ In their country's need./Their unconquered spirit/Strengthened the thin lines of gray./Their tender care was solace to the stricken./Reverence for God/And unfaltering faith in a righteous cause/Inspired heroism that survived/The immolation of sons/And courage that bore the agony of suspense/And the shock of disaster./The tragedy of the Confederacy may be forgotten/But the fruits of the noble service/Of the Daughters of the South/Are our perpetual heritage.*

The uniqueness of the South Carolina Confederate Women's Monument as a tribute to the fortitude of Southern women made it a popular location for women in the armed services during World War II. *Courtesy of South Carolina Confederate Relic Room and Military Museum.*

On the south side, the inscription continued:

> *At clouded dawn of peace/They faced the future/Undismayed by the problems/And fearless of the trials/In loving effort to heal/Their country's wounds/And with conviction/That from the ashes of ruin/Would come the resurrection/Of truth/With glorious vindication.*

Similar to the Fort Mill monument, the women's monument at the State House extolled the virtues of Southern womanhood, such as remaining true to God and country in the face of unimaginable circumstances. Additionally, these women served as model Christian wives and mothers. As sons should imitate the soldiers atop monuments, so daughters should emulate the qualities of these Confederate women.

Furthermore, the placement of the monument on the south side of the State House mirrored the northern location of the South Carolina Monument to Confederate soldiers. While praising the importance of creating the monument, an article in the *Confederate Veteran* about the unveiling contended,

> *Between these two memorials towers the Statehouse, the seat of South Carolina's sovereignty, the home of her greatness. It is an impressive picture, telling why South Carolina has so brilliant a past. It pictures that in life and in death her sons and her daughter, amidst all danger and all trouble, have gathered around her, ready to do and to die that she may live.*[125]

With the South Carolina Confederate Soldiers' and Women's Monuments anchoring the State House, the memorials affirmed the rightness of the Lost Cause in the Palmetto State's capital. It also placed the legacy of the Confederate years as a focal point in the state's history.

In addition to commemorating unique groups of South Carolinians, monuments were also erected to immortalize particular individuals. The forms of men in stone and bronze served as examples of individual heroism and embodied characteristics for the next generation to emulate. These monuments reminded future generations about the honor of their Confederate ancestors, which would hopefully guard against Northern biased interpretations of the war. Lee and Jackson served as popular heroes for the South to memorialize. South Carolinians, however, also included their own local champions.

Major General Wade Hampton was popularly regarded as Palmetto State's greatest Confederate hero and affectionately referred to as the state's Chieftain. In the opinion of many South Carolinians, he should be memorialized with the highest honors alongside the preeminent commanders from Virginia. Hampton furthered his standing through his postwar role in the Red Shirt movement as well as his subsequent election as governor, which ended Reconstruction in the state.

Until his health declined, Hampton played an active role in Confederate memorialization by assisting with the South Carolina Confederate Survivors' Association and speaking at Confederate Memorial Day ceremonies and monument unveilings. Having experienced Reconstruction, Hampton passionately desired for future generations to learn about the heroism of South Carolina's Confederate soldiers. Likewise, the ladies of the LMA and UDC believed that Hampton himself deserved the tributes of a grateful people. The earliest UDC chapter in Columbia took him as its namesake at its founding in 1896.

After his death on April 11, 1902, Hampton's reputation achieved legendary status. The SCV and UDC realized that it was time to establish a monument to this iconic South Carolinian. As part of the UDC's fundraising campaign, Malvina Gist Waring, Mrs. Ellison Capers and Mrs. Legare took ribbons from the flowers on the Chieftain's grave and made them into souvenirs to be sold for the benefit of the monument fund. Waring, caretaker of the

The pantheon fountain in honor of the six Confederate generals from Camden (1911). *Courtesy of Tommy Johnson and Keith Johnson.*

Confederate Monuments and Cemeteries of South Carolina

The Wade Hampton Monument in transport to the State House grounds. *Courtesy of South Carolina Confederate Relic Room and Military Museum.*

Confederate Relic Room and founder of the "Girls of the Sixties," placed one ribbon in the Relic Room's collection for safekeeping. Private efforts raised approximately $10,000. Meanwhile, newly elected Governor Duncan Heyward approved $20,000 in state funds for the monument.[126]

Appropriately, the monument portrays the gallant cavalier mounted on horseback surrounded by the names of some of his most famous battles. Designed by F. Wellington Ruckstuhl, the entire monument on its earthen mound and granite pedestal stands an impressive twenty-nine feet high. The monument faces northward as if to watch for Sherman's approach into the heart of the Palmetto State.

An estimated crowd of ten to fifteen thousand people gathered to observe the Hampton monument unveiling on November 20, 1906. The ceremony commenced with a parade of Confederate veterans, active militia and University of South Carolina students down Main Street to the State House. Immediately following the opening prayer by Reverend Ellison Capers, four of Hampton's grandchildren unveiled the monument. Appropriately, Hampton's longtime military and political companion, Major General M.C. Butler, delivered the dedication address. During the oration, he reminded all those gathered of the epic military accomplishments of the

Chieftain. Afterward, Charleston's German Artillery presented a nineteen-gun salute.[127]

In conjunction with the monuments to major Confederate generals, tributes were also constructed to honor privates and lower-level officers. One notable example is the memorialization surrounding Sergeant Richard Kirkland, a native of the Flat Rock area of Kershaw County. While serving in the Second South Carolina Infantry, Kirkland gained Southern and Northern prominence for his selfless acts at the Battle of Fredericksburg, Virginia. On December 14, 1862, Union troops repeatedly charged the Confederate defensive line, resulting in the horrific slaughter of the assaulting

A commemorative ribbon for the dedication of the Wade Hampton Monument in Columbia. *Courtesy of South Carolina Confederate Relic Room and Military Museum.*

Yankee soldiers. As the day progressed, some of the dying Union soldiers agonizingly pleaded for water. Unable to listen to the heart-wrenching pleas, Kirkland bounded over the breastworks and began to give the wounded enemy water from his canteen, earning him the nickname of "The Angel of Mayre's Heights."

The following September, Kirkland was killed in action at the Battle of Chickamauga. Kirkland's body was brought home and interred at White Oak Creek. A solemn wooden headboard with the initials "R.R.K." served as his temporary memorial. In 1909, the local John D. Kennedy UDC Chapter reburied Kirkland in the Camden Quaker Cemetery and erected a large monument in the shape of a boulder for his tombstone. Motivated by his selfless actions, individuals still leave canteens on his grave as a tribute to his actions at Fredericksburg.[128]

The citizens of Kershaw County desired a more prominent memorial to their local hero. Encouraged by school superintendent Dr. R.M. Kennedy, the schoolchildren of Camden contributed pennies to pay for a memorial fountain. Touched by the story and the schoolchildren's efforts, the National Humane Alliance of New York designed the fountain monument and assisted with costs associated with its assembly. In 1911, the monument was dedicated at the intersection of Broad and DeKalb Streets. The entire project cost $1,000. Due to increased automobile traffic, it was later moved to its current location in Hampton Park. Kirkland's prominent burial and interesting monument serve as a memorial to his actions but also as a reminder to future generations about the importance of heroic, selfless actions.[129]

In addition to these tributes, a monument in honor of Richard Kirkland was erected at the Fredericksburg Battlefield in 1964. Costing approximately $25,000, the monument was erected by the State of South Carolina, the Commonwealth of Virginia and the Richard Rowland Kirkland Memorial Foundation, composed of Kirkland family members. Telling his story to all those who visit the battlefield, the monument consists of a large bronze sculpture of Kirkland giving water to a fallen Yankee who lays upon a granite base.[130]

In cemeteries and church burial grounds across the Palmetto State, additional powerful stories regarding the legacy of the burial of individual Confederate soldiers remain evident. Previous chapters have discussed reburial and commemoration of groups of soldiers. However, stories of the individual soldiers are located in nearly every cemetery in the Palmetto State. Gravestone inscriptions can reveal a person's belief system, lifetime achievements or important family relations. No matter the simplicity or the elaborate nature of the gravestone, ultimately they serve as the final

Above: The grave of Richard Kirkland in Quaker Cemetery, Camden. Kirkland's remains were relocated here in 1909. One year later, the local John D. Kennedy Chapter of the UDC erected the memorial stone. Today, visitors inspired by Kirkland's actions leave canteens in his honor. *Courtesy of Kristina and Tommy Johnson.*

Left: Local schoolchildren raised money for a fountain monument to honor Richard Kirkland (1911). The monument has spouts on both the northern and southern sides in order to symbolize his heroic action of giving the enemy water at the Battle of Fredericksburg. *Courtesy of Kristina and Tommy Johnson.*

reminder of a life departed and the mortality of humanity. Occasionally, in lieu of reclaiming fallen soldiers' bodies when resources or circumstances would not allow, families erected memorial stones in their local cemetery. This practice allowed families to have a nearby "tomb" to commemorate the sacrifice of their loved one.

The inability to properly care for and inter the remains of spouses and sons created lasting bitterness, as evidenced by Lieutenant Joseph Friedeberg's memorial in Elmwood Cemetery. Erected by his mourning widow, the monument tells the story of Friedeberg's death at Middletown, Maryland, in the "hands of the enemy" from wounds received during the Sharpsburg Campaign in September of 1862. The inscription poignantly continues, "Alone and friendless on the soil,/Thy blood was shed to save,/Thy soul hath found its father's god/Thy heart a stranger's grave." Haunted by the loss of her beloved and her inability to reclaim his body, the passage of time failed to heal his widow's suffering. Evidenced by the elaborate tribute, she earnestly desired for future generations to remember her husband's life and the reason for his untimely death.

Nearby in Elmwood Cemetery, another family in mourning placed a simple memorial obelisk to their son, J. Thornwell Scott, who was killed during the second day of fighting at Gettysburg. His fate is simply inscribed on the obelisk: "Killed at Gettysburg. His body was not recovered." The solemn memorial stands alone in a wrought-iron fence enclosure as a lasting tribute to a beloved son's death and his unclaimed remains.

Even those who were able to reclaim their dead often felt the need to elaborately describe the cause and place of death. Many inscriptions also promised to never forget their fallen soldier. Only twenty-three years old, John J. McKain died in April of 1862, during the Peninsula Campaign. Comforted by the words of Father Abram Joseph Ryan's poem, "C.S.A.," his family determined to etch them into the gravestone. Today, visitors to Camden's Quaker Cemetery are greeted by the reminder of sacrifice and sorrow: "Fresh tears shall fall forever o'er all who died while wearing the gray."[131]

Many Confederate War survivors spent the remaining years of their lives striving to honor their fallen comrades through reasserting the rightness of the Lost Cause and struggling to reclaim political power from Northern Republicans. Haunted by the memories of the war and sometimes burdened by their own survival, some even struggled through delusional episodes of refighting the war while on their deathbeds. Calling out commands as life faded from their bodies, officers attempted to lead the memories of men into battle. Such was the case of Colonel Thomas Glascock Bacon of the

Captain Paul Hamilton's grave at St. Helena Episcopal Church in Beaufort. Only twenty years old, Hamilton was killed in action on December 29, 1862, near Vicksburg. Utilizing popular South Carolina symbolism for soldier graves, Hamilton's grave has a relief of a cannon tube, fallen flag and a palmetto tree. *Courtesy of Kristina and Tommy Johnson.*

The grave of States Rights Gist located at Trinity Episcopal Church, Columbia. Gist was killed at the fierce fighting at Franklin, Tennessee. Utilizing Victorian symbolism, the grave has a broken pillar crowned with a laurel wreath, representing a life cut short but still crowned with glory. *Courtesy of Kristina and Tommy Johnson.*

Lieutenant Colonel Benjamin Johnson's grave in Magnolia Cemetery. Johnson, of Hampton's Legion, was killed at the First Battle of Manassas. A common symbol on cavalrymen's gravestones, a sheathed saber rests across the tomb, representing that the fight is finished for these brave cavaliers. *Courtesy of Kristina and Tommy Johnson.*

The grave of William H. Brunson, Old Village Cemetery (Willowbrook Cemetery), Edgefield. His family poignantly inscribed on the headstone, "Goodnight, brave soldier, sleep, thy work is done." *Courtesy of Kristina and Tommy Johnson.*

C.W. Hudgins wanted to be remembered by one attribute—he was a Confederate soldier. His grave is located in Mount Hope Cemetery, Florence. *Courtesy of Kristina and Tommy Johnson.*

Seventh South Carolina Infantry when he died in 1876. Realizing he had finally gone to a "happier camping ground," his family decided to inscribe his last words on his grave. With his dying breath, Bacon cried out,

Let me go! I want to go to my regiment![132]

CHAPTER 7

"THAT WE HAVE A RIGHT TO BE HERE"

South Carolina Monuments on a National Level

This is one of the places owned and controlled by the United States Government, linked to the memory of great Confederate struggles, where we good old Confederates are made to feel that we are entirely at home. That we have a right to be here. That we have a perfect right to erect a monument to the valor of South Carolina's Confederate soldiery by the very side of one to the gallant men who upheld the Stars and Stripes. Brother Confederate Veterans, you will see on this battlefield what none of us, as we went sadly home in 1865, ever dreamed of seeing. Witness the splendid monuments to our fallen Confederate brigade commanders, erected by the United States Government. And when you look at similar monuments to the fallen Union Generals you will find not a particle of difference. The Confederate and Union hero has been treated alike.
—General C. Irvine Walker, Chickamauga South Carolina Monument Dedication, 1901[133]

On May 27, 1901, General C. Irvine Walker stood before a crowd on the battlefield of Chickamauga to dedicate a monument to the soldiers from the Palmetto State. The speakers for the day, many of whom were Confederate veterans who had fought on these very same fields, stood in awe of the reconciliatory overtures offered by the federal government. Forty years after the start of the war, the first South Carolina Confederate monument was dedicated on the battlefield where much of the killing and dying had actually occurred.

Since the close of the war, battlefields had primarily been controlled by the Grand Army of the Republic (GAR), which was the Union veteran organization, and Union preservation groups. Due to this practice, most Confederate monuments had been formally and informally banned. In 1887, the GAR determined "that no local post should support the erection of monuments in honor of the men who distinguished themselves by their services in the cause of treason and rebellion." Furthermore, many former Confederates did not desire to create battlefield memorials, since they perceived those fields as symbols of their military defeat. Around the turn of the century, LMA and UDC organizations realized that battlefields would allow people from all over the country, not just fellow Southerners, to reflect on the Lost Cause and the heroics of the Confederate dead. When the War Department and later the National Park Service took possession of the major battlefields, the dedication of Confederate monuments was finally allowed within set guidelines. Chickamauga had the distinction of becoming the first federally preserved battlefield on April 19, 1890.[134]

The South Carolina monument dedicated at Chickamauga in 1901 was the state's first monument on a national battlefield. The Stewart Stone Company of Columbia furnished the stone for the base. The monument design has bronze figures of an infantry soldier actively loading his rifle and an artillerist with sponge in hand gazing off into the distance to see where his shot landed. Symbolic of the state's military heritage, the monument was topped off with a thirteen-foot-high bronze palmetto tree. When finished, the monument stood an imposing thirty-three feet and five inches high. In 1905, due to the weak structure of the bronze palmetto fronds, the tree was removed and replaced with a granite obelisk.[135]

Before the monument was unveiled, the band struck up "Bonnie Blue Flag" and Bishop Ellison Capers, with tears in his eyes, addressed the crowd: "They live in memory: they live in history: they are with us in our Monuments, to refine our selfishness, to purify our ambitions, to chasten our hopes, and to exalt our comrades." Afterward, he introduced four South Carolina girls to remove the curtain covering the monument. Each of the girls represented a group of the state's troops that had fought at the battle: Elberta Bland, granddaughter of Lieutenant Colonel Elbert Bland, who died at the battle, represented Kershaw's Brigade; Ada Orie Walker, granddaughter of General Walker, represented Manigault's Brigade; Mary Syndor Dupre, grand-niece of Colonel Clement Henry Stevens, who was mortally wounded during the battle, represented Gist's Brigade; and Elizabeth Teague represented Culpepper's Brigade.[136]

Interestingly, this monument and the dedication ceremony contained characteristics that expressed both vindication and reconciliation sentiments. The soldiers on the monument remain in the active stance of fighting—these were not the passive parade rest soldiers. However, the Confederate veterans and South Carolina citizens involved in the project were astounded by the willingness of the War Department to allow them to memorialize fallen Confederates on federal property. Not a single dedication speech promoted further hostilities or bitterness between the North and the South. In his dedication address, General Henry V. Boynton pondered in astonishment:

The dedication of the Chickamauga South Carolina Monument. In 1905, the bronze palmetto was replaced with a granite obelisk. *Courtesy of Camden Archives and Museum.*

It will give emphasis to these most remarkable surroundings if we try for a moment to picture to ourselves the universal bewilderment of those great hosts who on this vast battlefield gave their lives for their convictions, if at the command of some prophet of this new day they should rise and confront each other in their splendid ranks again…What would they say to each other as they learned fact after fact of this park project?…If the fallen heroes of South Carolina…should come upon this gathering, would their amazement be lessened to find the authorities of South Carolina, the banner State of their great war, and crowds of its citizens and Veterans welcomed by the National Government…dedicating a monument to tell to the ages the proud story of their own heroism in battle? How could we explain this scene to these heroes whose eyes closed in death a generation ago while this field was rocking in the convulsions of tremendous civil war?[137]

Perhaps no other South Carolina monument better typifies the transition into reconciliation and reunion than the Chickamauga monument. The designers of the monument still remembered the horrors of the war, the difficulties of Reconstruction and the rebuilding before the turn of the century. Nevertheless, the reconciliatory overture by the federal government to allow the memorialization of the valor of their fallen comrades helped the healing process and left the attendees in awe of the circumstances.

Those who gathered to dedicate the South Carolina monument at Chickamauga were quick to recognize the difference between the treatment that they received from the War Department at Chickamauga and the GAR-controlled lands at Gettysburg, where no Confederate state monuments had

In 1913, Lieutenant Moses Wood of the Fifteenth South Carolina Infantry revisited the Chickamauga battlefield and posed for a picture on the steps of the South Carolina monument with his two children. Battlefield monuments provided a place for veterans to reflect on their service and remember their fallen comrades. *Courtesy of James Clary.*

yet been erected. During the dedication at Chickamauga, the problems of Gettysburg surfaced as General Walker announced that Chickamauga "should be more than Gettysburg with its monuments along one side alone; the lines of both armies should be equally marked."[138] In fact, at the time of the South Carolina Chickamauga monument dedication, the land comprising the main Confederate line at Gettysburg had not even been purchased for preservation and memorialization; only the Union line had been adequately preserved.[139]

Almost immediately after the Battle of Gettysburg, the Gettysburg Battlefield Memorial Association (GBMA) began to purchase battlefield land. In its charter, the GBMA clearly stated that its mission was to commemorate and memorialize only the Union side of the battle—not the Confederate. The organization experienced financial difficulties. In 1880, the GAR decided to assume control of the organization by acquiring a majority stake and electing its members to the GBMA governing board. The GAR furthered the mission of the GBMA to preserve and memorialize the battlefield. Its efforts relied heavily on financial support by individual states, which further promoted the purchase and preservation of Union battle lines.[140]

At this time, there was also a growing interest for the federal government to assume a more prominent role with funding and supporting the project. With many GAR members being adamantly opposed to any aspect of Confederate memorialization, this quickly became a politically charged issue. Meanwhile, not all contemporary historians of the battle believed that the Confederate line should be ignored. In November of 1889, John Bachelder, who is considered the first scholar of the Battle of Gettysburg, asserted:

> *Yet, if Congress desires that the Confederate positions be preserved, on that celebrated field, not by elaborate monuments, but by enduring historic tablets, the data exists for laying out the battle-lines and marking the continuous positions of troops upon them…As only the positions of one side are marked, it really possesses no tactical value whatsoever.*

Bachelder believed that it was imperative to the history of the battle to mark both sides in order to present the battlefield to visitors as "the most wonderful object-map in the world." He knew that without Congressional support for funding the project it would be impossible to accomplish. As a consolation to the GAR, he solely wished for markers of Confederate positions, not elaborate commemorative monuments.[141]

Starting in 1886, a handful of Confederate markers were allowed, but only under strict guidelines enacted by the GBMA and the GAR. These guidelines

General Wade Hampton revisited the Gettysburg battlefield as a senator on July 13, 1886. As part of the delegation, he helped to outline his movements at East Cavalry Field, where he had been wounded on July 3, 1863. While serving as a senator, Hampton attempted to promote the development of the Confederate side of the battle's history and became a supporter of John Bachelder. *Courtesy of Dale Molina.*

included only erecting historic markers on locations where Confederate regiments formed their attacks during the three days of the battle—not where the actual fighting occurred. Furthermore, the GMBA restricted any monument that might glorify the Confederate Cause and had final approval over content and location. Markers contained historical information about troop movement and strength; they did not contain interpretive information to impart meaning, which could be viewed as memorializing the Southern Cause. Under these restrictions, most Southerners avoided donating funds toward Gettysburg commemorative causes or rallying to change the system. Instead, they continued memorializing their loved ones in local counties and cemeteries, where they could mourn and remember away from the authority of the GAR or the federal government.

The issue of Confederate memorialization and the political force of the GAR continued to plague politicians when they considered accepting Gettysburg under the control of the federal government. In 1890, the same year the War Department assumed control of Chickamauga, Congress defeated a measure to have the government additionally annex Gettysburg. Ultimately, the War Department took over management of the battlefield on February 11, 1895. With federal assistance, the project to mark the spot of Confederate positions moved forward. Even with these markers, however, the political force of the GAR still limited the design and location of where these tablets were to be erected. Colonel William Oates, who had led the Fifteenth Alabama Infantry, went to his grave in 1910 after fighting with the GAR for eight years over the placement of his regiment's advance markers. He firmly expressed that his regiment's marker should be positioned behind the Twentieth Maine Infantry monument, which Brevet Major General Joshua Chamberlain and the GAR were adamantly against.[142]

Despite the difficulties created by the GAR and the GBMA concerning Southern memorialization, contemporary events around the turn of the century began to popularize ideas of reconciliation and a common American identity. On June 16, 1896, an editorial in the *Gettysburg Compiler* argued that it was now appropriate to

> [tell] *the story of American heroism on both sides of that memorable struggle; and surely after a generation has passed away, there can be no sectional passions to interpose objections to making the monuments and statues of Gettysburg tell the whole story of the matchless courage of American soldiers, whether they fought under the stars and stripes or under the stars and bars…Lee and his lieutenants should be preserved in imposing statues on the Confederate lines…Let us now invite the South to complete the historic lesson of Gettysburg by placing the statues of her chieftains corresponding with the statues of the Union heroes, and let all stand to tell to future generations the story of American heroism.*[143]

Of the three Southern monuments dedicated on the Gettysburg battlefield between 1886 and 1917, only one of these monuments commemorated a regiment, the Second Maryland Infantry (Confederate First Maryland Infantry). The two other monuments marked where General Armistead was mortally wounded and the symbolic "High Water Mark" of the Confederacy. The "High Water Mark" monument could barely be considered a Confederate monument, as it had been paid for by Northern states as a memorial to their ability to ebb the Confederate attack. Not one Southern state gave money for this monument.[144]

In 1917, Virginia dedicated the first Confederate state monument at Gettysburg. The state had petitioned for a monument in 1908, but it was vehemently rejected by the GBMA due to pressure from a local GAR. It took until 1982 for all of the Confederate states to be memorialized on the Northern battlefield.[145]

Northern authoritative attitudes and the resulting difficulties soured many Confederates on Gettysburg. Instead, they continued to focus on their local counties and other battlefields. Prominent battlefields, such as Shiloh, Vicksburg and Chickamauga, were more amenable to the Southerners, possibly because these battlefields were located in the South and therefore were not constrained by local GARs. Outside of Chickamauga, South Carolina dedicated monuments at Winchester Stonewall Cemetery (1879), two monuments at Petersburg (1890) and one at Vicksburg (1935). Additionally, the Palmetto State's UDC chapters raised money for the Confederate monument at Shiloh (1917) as well as the Richmond monuments for Robert E. Lee (1890) and Jefferson Davis (1907). Due to difficulties with the GAR and the availability of memorialization at other locations, many Southerners abandoned monumentation at Gettysburg until the overall passion and financial resources for monumentation had severely dwindled.[146]

The approaching centennial of the war triggered a resurgence of interest in Confederate heritage. As part of the commemorations, the South Carolina Confederate War Centennial Commission formed the Gettysburg Memorial Committee. Both the commission and the committee members consisted of politicians, Sons of Confederate Veterans (SCV) and UDC members. Together, they determined to finally dedicate a monument for the soldiers from the Palmetto State on the long-neglected Gettysburg battlefield.

At 4:30 p.m. on July 2, 1963, almost exactly to the time of the 100th anniversary of the deadly assault of Kershaw's Brigade, South Carolinians gathered to dedicate a monument to all of the Palmetto State's soldiers who had fought during the Gettysburg Campaign. The ceremony included the members of the South Carolina Confederate Centennial Commission and South Carolina Gettysburg Memorial Committee. Governor Donald S. Russell Jr. presented the dedicatory address. In a definite shift from the earlier practice of having monument unveilings performed by veterans or young ladies, symbolizing the innocence and purity of the Lost Cause, Governor Russell and Representative John A. May, chairman of the Centennial Commission, unveiled the monument. These deviations from traditional dedication ceremonies reflect an overall shift away from a passive handing down of the torch to the next generation. Monument dedications had often been affected by national politics and remembrance issues, and the Gettysburg monument proved not to be an exception. Civil War Centennial events often reflected the problems of 1960s desegregation and defensive

Above: The monument to the Confederate dead at the Battle of Rivers Bridge, South Carolina, dedicated in 1878. *Courtesy of South Carolina Confederate Relic Room and Military Museum.*

Right: The program from the Robert E. Lee Monument Association dedication ceremonies. *Courtesy of South Carolina Confederate Relic Room and Military Museum.*

The Gettysburg South Carolina monument dedicated during the centennial of the battle. *Courtesy of Kristina Johnson.*

political posturing. Consequently, the sacrifice of the Confederate soldiers becomes lost with the dedication and inscription of the South Carolina Gettysburg monument.

At first glance, the Gettysburg monument design is similar to slab monuments constructed within the Palmetto State after 1922. Furthermore, it includes an interactive element of two benches, beckoning visitors to pause and remember the sacrifice on the nearby fields. On its front face, the monument recognizes the units that participated at the battle. However, the reverse of the monument lists the individual members of the commissions that supported the project. In some instances, certain individuals were on both committees and therefore their names were inscribed on the monument twice. This inscription differs from previous monuments that had solely credited just the local LMA, UDC, local government, the State of South Carolina or sometimes one major financial contributor (usually a Confederate veteran). This area on the monument could have been used to list soldiers' names, South Carolina casualty figures or even descriptions of the brave actions of the men during the three days of fighting. Instead, the space is used to honor individual members from modern committees—not the Confederate soldiers who actually fought and died. Listing each modern contributor in place of other possible inscriptions portrays more of a tribute for the modern South Carolina Confederate Centennial Commission and South Carolina Gettysburg Memorial Committee rather than a simple and fitting tribute to the men who wore the gray.

Confederate Monuments and Cemeteries of South Carolina

Presently, Northern and Southern monument associations continue to assert their versions of Civil War history and tend to memorialize their dead on the battlefields instead of courthouse squares. In the spring of 2009, South Carolinians will gather at Spotsylvania's Bloody Angle to dedicate the first monument to McGowan's Brigade. The effort, spearheaded by the Samuel McGowan SCV Camp #40, commemorates the approximately twenty hours of fierce hand-to-hand combat engaged in by 1,300 South Carolinians, resulting in 451 casualties.[147]

On these battlefields of national importance, regardless of political overtones or design, these monuments symbolize the efforts of the state's regiments on the field of combat. For many soldiers, there could be no higher honor. Both Union and Confederate monuments on these fields of battle remind modern visitors of the lives forever changed and lost on these hallowed grounds. These visitors remember that the cornfields and tree lines are not simply picturesque countryside vistas; instead, they were places where people fought, suffered and died for their beliefs.

The modern battlefield visitor will often pause at the monuments to take pictures and sometimes leave small tokens of affection, such as flags, wreaths and pennies. Internalizing and identifying with stories of battlefield heroism and tragedy, most visitors leave with a sense of respect for the wartime generation. The difficulties overcome while erecting these monuments have long since been forgotten by most Americans; but imagine the tragedy of these battlefields without fitting tributes to those who served on both sides. The story would be incomplete and would leave lingering feelings of one side being wronged by the other. Instead, national battlefields serve as a memorial to all soldiers. Even in 1901, with the memory of the war and Reconstruction still fresh, General Walker understood the need for common places of commemoration in order to promote the healing of America. As he eloquently dedicated the Chickamauga monument, overwhelmed by the meaning of the moment on a grander scale, Walker breathlessly affirmed,

The monument which South Carolina erected and today unveils stands an immortal tribute, not only to the valor of her sons who fought on this historic battlefield, but to the peace and harmony which now blesses our land.[148]

"THE RUINS OF OUR BURIED HOPES"

We have rebuilt on the ruins of our buried hopes…We poor "Rebels" have found new homes, new hopes, and we strive to forget the bitterness of defeat. But memory often carries us back over the bloody chasm to that other life, to commune in those then happy homes with loved ones now absent and dead.
—Margaret Crawford Adams, 1903[149]

Memory, as Margaret Crawford Adams poignantly explained to her grandchildren, lingers as both haunting and comforting. The powerful pull of past memories proved inescapable. No matter the pain, Adams wanted her memories to play a critical role in teaching her grandchildren about the impact of the war. She was not alone in her thoughts. In an introduction to his poem "A Land Without Ruins," Father Abram Joseph Ryan declared, "A land without ruins is a land without memories—a land without memories is a land without history." If this is true, then one must first embrace remembering in order to create enduring history. Yet memory is not stable. It is continually shaped by the progression of time. Each generation passes those memories to the next, hoping to retain the lessons and truth through time. New generations confront their own challenges, which can alter their interpretation of memories. Each generation changes the meaning of memories in the wake of contemporary events while including their own interpretations.

South Carolinians, like other citizens living in the former Confederate states, altered forms of monumentation based upon national and local events. Using stone and bronze, they demonstrated what aspects of national reconciliation they would accept. Likewise, their decisions shaped national and regional trends in Civil War memory. During Reconstruction, South Carolinians busied themselves with trying to earn enough to live, avoiding problems with the federal occupation force and gathering Confederate

The new and old graves of Alexander Tynes in Elmwood Cemetery, demonstrating the different generations of commemorating Confederate soldiers. *Courtesy of Kristina and Tommy Johnson.*

dead. The monuments gave tangibility to mourning the Confederate dead, yet they also masked an underlying sentiment of resentment. Defiant soldier stances and engravings on the monuments dedicated between 1878 and 1903 served as an outlet for South Carolinians to release their anger. The patriotic spirit surrounding the Spanish-American War helped to ease these tensions, but individuals still decided what aspects of reconciliation would be acceptable. These passionate and vitriolic statements gradually faded as the South began to embrace a new nationalism. The monuments dedicated between 1904 and 1922 reflected the feelings of reconciliation through the use of soldiers at parade rest in the public sphere. After 1922, the importance of monuments shifted to national-level remembrances and simplistic slab designs.

Confederate monumentation within South Carolina started as a private method of mourning loved ones lost during the war, transformed into a public statement of resistance and then represented a symbol of the new nationalism. Today, most Confederate monuments in front of county courthouses stand alongside monuments dedicated to soldiers of the Spanish-American War, Great War, World War II, Korea and Vietnam. Perhaps these monuments

"The Ruins of Our Buried Hopes"

The 2008 Confederate Memorial Day services at Mount Hope Cemetery in Florence. *Courtesy of Tommy Johnson.*

will one day be joined by monuments and memorials to South Carolinians who served in the Gulf War and the War on Terror.

The ritualized mourning and memorialization patterns established by previous generations of South Carolinians continue to impact how we remember the war. On Confederate Memorial Day, Palmetto State citizens still gather at local cemeteries or monuments for commemoration ceremonies. Taking the commemorative patterns passed down through the generations, modern memorializers present wreaths, place flags on graves, play music and eulogize the bravery of the Southern solider. Thus, modern generations continue to utilize the places and activities established by their ancestors as the proper way to commemorate the Confederate soldiers.

The funeral of the third CSS *Hunley* crew provides a recent example of employing the same traditions of mourning and memory as the first generation of commemorators. The mission to create a submarine to weaken the Union blockade on Charleston began in 1863. Over the next few months, two crews would die attempting to perfect the *Hunley*'s warfare capabilities. The first crew was initially buried in the local mariners' cemetery. The second crew was buried along the banks of the Cooper

River marsh in Magnolia Cemetery. On February 17, 1864, the third crew of the *Hunley* made maritime history by becoming the first submarine to sink an enemy ship, the USS *Housatonic*. After signaling its achievement, the *Hunley* sank—its story and crew lost until being discovered in 1995. In 2000, the first crew was reburied alongside the second crew. That same year, the submarine was raised from the Atlantic Ocean and sent for conservation. In the process, the remains of the third eight-man crew were also recovered.

Known as the "Last Confederate Funeral," the eight-man crew of the *Hunley* was laid to rest with full military honors in Magnolia Cemetery on April 17, 2004. The funeral commenced with a ceremony at White Point Gardens, located on the famous Charleston Battery. The setting provided a nearby view of the Charleston Harbor, including Fort Sumter and Fort Moultrie. Through generations of commemoration, the landscape was already appropriately graced with maritime Confederate monuments and memorial cannons. As speakers eulogized the men and their brave actions, the eight wooden coffins rested peacefully under the shadow of the Defenders of Charleston Confederate Monument (1932). Onlookers, many dressed in period attire, wore black armbands out of respect for Victorian mourning customs.

After the early morning ceremony, horse-drawn caissons and pallbearers embarked on a four-and-a-half-mile processional to Magnolia Cemetery. The processional included dignitaries and reenactors, including hundreds of reenactors dressed as widows. The solemn clacking of the horse hooves on the barely altered Charleston streetscape caused the bustling, modern city to pause, if only for a moment.

Once arriving in Magnolia Cemetery, the event assumed a more somber tone. Nestled around the base of the Charleston Confederate Monument, mourners filed in to sit in the neatly placed folding chairs tucked between the gravestones of the Confederate section. Onlookers assembled among the known and unknown soldiers in gray, silently reflecting on the sacrifice of the soldiers resting underneath their feet. The city of the dead seemed alive with memories. One could almost hear Henry Timrod's "Ode" or Reverend Girardeau's solemn pronouncement upon the reburial of the Gettysburg dead: "Shoulder to shoulder they stood; now let them lie side by side. Confederates in life, confederates let them be in death."

During the formal funeral ceremony, dignitaries eulogized about the rightness of honoring the eight men. The orators discussed the bravery of the men who decided to serve in the risky submarine, despite the loss of the previous two crews. The importance of the *Hunley* to modern naval

"The Ruins of Our Buried Hopes"

The funeral service for the third *Hunley* crew at Magnolia Cemetery. *Courtesy of Kristina Johnson.*

history was also discussed. Several of the orators reminded onlookers of the religious implications of the transient nature of life and the Biblical promise of an afterlife. Tears were shed on this sacred burial place once again as the profound realization became apparent—this was a real funeral.

Concluding the ceremonies, pallbearers carried the eight coffins from the Confederate section to the *Hunley* plot. After a prayer and the playing of taps, the coffins were lowered into a trench-style grave beside the first two *Hunley* crews. Descendants of the crew and other mourners threw roses into the open ground. Other onlookers threw a handful of dust in reminder of Genesis 3:19, "For dust you are, and to dust you shall return."

Despite the changes in memorialization, South Carolinians have continued to gather near the places made sacred by their forbearers. Although meanings and implications surrounding the commemoration of the Confederate soldier and the Southern Cause have shifted over time, these changes have become part of the intricate layers of history. By studying these transformations, a greater understanding of the South Carolina story emerges. Nevertheless, one aspect of Confederate legacy will always remain—the Confederate soldier himself. As his story takes on new meaning, each generation clings to the "memory of the Southern soldier—the ideal hero of a hero-worshiping people."[150]

Remains of the *Hunley* crew being laid to rest at Magnolia Cemetery. *Courtesy of Kristina Johnson.*

There's a grandeur in graves—there's a glory in gloom;
For out of the gloom future brightness is born,
As after the night, looms the sunrise of morn;
And the graves of the dead, with the grass overgrown,
May yet form the footstool of Liberty's throne;
And each single wreck in the warpath of Might
Shall yet be a rock in the Temple of Right.[151]

NOTES

ABBREVIATIONS
SCCRRMM: South Carolina Confederate Relic Room and Military Museum
GNMP: Gettysburg National Military Park
CMMSC: *Confederate Monuments and Markers in South Carolina* (unpublished, available at the SCCRRMM)

INTRODUCTION
1. "Ceremonies at the Unveiling of the SC Monument on the Chickamauga Battlefield, May 27th, 1901. Together with a Record of the Commission who Suggested and Were Instrumental in Securing and Erecting the Monument, Etc.," 36, SCCRRMM.
2. E.B. Whitman, ed. "Remarks on National Cemeteries.—Original Military Division of the Tennessee"; Executive Committee for the Army Reunion, *The Army Reunion: With Reports of the Meetings of the Societies of the Army of the Cumberland; the Army of the Tennessee; the Army of the Ohio; and the Army of Georgia* (Chicago: S.C. Griggs & Co., 1869), 226.
3. Margaret Crawford Adams, ed., "Tales of a Grandmother, or, Recollections of the Confederate War"; State Committee Daughters of the Confederacy, *South Carolina Women in the Confederacy* (Columbia: The State Company, 1903), 1:210–11.

CHAPTER 1
4. Letter from Henry P. Farrow to Richard Franklin Simpson, 29 September 1863, in Guy R. Everson and Edward W. Simpson Jr., eds., *"Far, Far from Home": The Wartime Letters of Dick and Tally Simpson, 3rd South Carolina Volunteers* (New York: Oxford University Press, 1994), 282–89.

5. Letter from Taliaferro N. Simpson to Anna Talullah Simpson, 25 December 1862, in Everson and Edward, *"Far, Far from Home,"* 168–70.

6. Letter from Henry P. Farrow to Richard Franklin Simpson, 29 September 1863, in Everson and Edward, *"Far, Far from Home,"* 288–89, 296; Capt. John Hames Chapter UDC, Jonesville, SC, "The Confederate Dead at Old Stone Church and at Pendleton," *Recollections and Reminiscences, 1861–1865, through World War I* (South Carolina United Daughters of the Confederacy, 1997), 7:381; letter from Taliaferro N. Simpson to Anna Talullah Simpson, September 24, 1862, in Everson and Edward, *"Far, Far from Home,"* 150–51.

7. Mrs. M.S. Williams, "Woman's Work at Pendleton, 1901," in *South Carolina Women in the Confederacy*, 34.

8. Mrs. Joseph Marshall, "Woman's Work at Abbeville, 1901," in *South Carolina Women in the Confederacy*, 69.

9. Mrs. Campbell Bryce, "Reminiscences, 1897," in *South Carolina Women in the Confederacy*, 83.

10. Elmwood Cemetery National Register Nomination, National Park Service, 1996; 1924 Memorial Pamphlet, Elmwood Cemetery Record Series, SCCRRMM.

11. Elmwood Cemetery Burial List, Correspondence, and 1924 Memorial Pamphlet, Elmwood Cemetery Record Series, SCCRRMM; *The State*, January 6, 1985.

12. Historic Greenville Foundation and City of Greenville Parks and Recreation, "Springwood Cemetery: A Historical Tour," pamphlet, City of Greenville; Springwood Cemetery Master Plan, 2003.

13. Samuel Weaver, "Soldiers' National Cemetery: Report to David Willis, Esquire Agent for A.G. Curtin, Governor of Pennsylvania," GNMP, Vertical Files, "Confederate Reinterments," 7-22 PC.

14. Gregory A. Coco, *Strange and Blighted Land, Gettysburg: The Aftermath of a Battle* (Gettysburg: Thomas Publicans, 1995), 80–141.

15. Ibid.

16. "The Rebel Dead," *Star-Sentinel*, February 2, 1864; GNMP Vertical Files, "Confederate Reinterments," 7-16 PC.

17. Gregory Coco, "Where Defeated Valor Lies: A Rose Farm Mystery Solved," *Gettysburg Magazine* 30 (2004): 118.

18. "Calhoun's Remains," *New York Times*, November 22, 1884.

19. James J. Baldwin III, *The Struck Eagle: A Biography of Brigadier General Micah Jenkins, and a History of the Fifth South Carolina Volunteers and the Palmetto Sharpshooters* (Shippensburg, PA: Burd Street Press, 1996), 364–65.

20. William A. Nicholson, "Burying the Dead," *Recollections and Reminiscences,*

6:324–25; letter from Jane A. Doogan to Mrs. Swindell, 16 April 1926, Elmwood Cemetery Record Series, SCCRRMM.

21. Letter from Taliaferro N. Simpson to Anna Talullah Simpson, 24 September 1862, in Everson and Edward, *"Far, Far from Home,"* 150–51.

CHAPTER 2

22. Letter from Mary J. Dogan to John S. Palmer, 16 June 1870, in Louis P. Towles, ed., *A World Turned Upside Down: The Palmers of South Santee, 1818–1881* (Columbia: University of South Carolina Press, 1996), 650.

23. P.G. Palmer, "An Incident of Second Manassas," *Confederate Veteran* 21 (1913): 169; Mrs. J.E. Alexander, "Visiting Manassas Battlefield," *Confederate Veteran* 4 (1896): 380.

24. Palmer, "An Incident of Second Manassas," 169; Alexander, "Visiting Manassas Battlefield," 380.

25. Palmer, "An Incident of Second Manassas," 169; Alexander, "Visiting Manassas Battlefield," 380.

26. Letter from Esther Simons Palmer to Elizabeth Palmer Porcher, August 1870, in Towles, *A World Turned Upside Down*, 660–61; Palmer, "An Incident of Second Manassas," 169; Alexander, "Visiting Manassas Battlefield," 380.

27. Michael Kammen, *Mystic Cords of Memory: The Transformation of Tradition in American Culture* (New York: Knopf, 1991), 103; Mildred Lewis Rutherford, "History of the Ladies Memorial Associations: Monuments to the Confederate Soldiers," *Miss Rutherford's Scrap Book: Valuable Information about the South*, 2 (Athens: Mildred Lewis Rutherford, April 1924); Mrs. Charles J. Williams, *Columbus Times*, March 12, 1866.

28. Gaines M. Foster, *Ghosts of the Confederacy: Defeat, the Lost Cause, and the Emergence of the New South 1865 to 1913* (New York and Oxford: Oxford University Press, 1987), 39–45; Alice A. Gaillard Palmer, "Ladies Memorial Association, Charleston, South Carolina," Confederated Southern Memorial Association, in *History of the Confederated Memorial Associations of the South* (New Orleans: Graham Press, 1904), 241.

29. Mildred Lewis Rutherford, "History of the Ladies Memorial Assciations," 9.

30. Marshall, "Woman's Work at Abbeville, 1901," in South Carolina *Women in the Confederacy*, 69.

31. Charleston News and Courier, December 1, 1882; Palmer, "Ladies Memorial Association, Charleston, South Carolina," in *History of the Confederated Memorial Associations of the South*, 241–42.

32. Palmer, "Ladies Memorial Association, Charleston, South Carolina," in *History of the Confederated Memorial Associations of the South*, 241–42.

33. Mrs. B.D. M'Leod, "The First Confederate Monument," *Confederate Veteran* 8 (1905): 11; R.B. Haughton, "First Confederate Monuments Erected," *Confederate Veteran* 19 (1911): 233; Virginia C. Tarrh, "Women's Work at Cheraw, October 6, 1898," in *South Carolina Women in the Confederacy*, 29; Frances Stricklin and Bessie Page, "Cheraw," in *Confederate Monuments and Markers in South Carolina*, 1, unpublished manuscript, SCCRRMM.

34. Article from the Cheraw *Chronicle*, May 7, 1903, reprinted in M'Leod, "The First Confederate Monument," 11.

35. M'Leod, "The First Confederate Monument," 11; Haughton, "First Confederate Monuments Erected," 233; Tarrh, "Women's Work at Cheraw," in *South Carolina Women in the Confederacy*, 29; Stricklin and Page, "Cheraw," CMMSC, SCCRRMM. The Indian Mound Cemetery at Romney, West Virginia, claims to be the first Confederate monument, but theirs was not dedicated until September of 1867, two months after Cheraw. Further arguments have been made that a monument in Missouri was the first Confederate monument; however, the claim has been refined that it is the first Confederate monument west of the Mississippi River. Major E.H. McDonald, "First Confederate Monument," *Confederate Veteran* 19 (1911): 372–73.

36. M'Leod, "The First Confederate Monument," 11; Rutherford, "History of the Ladies Memorial Associations," 9.

37. J.H. Hudson, "Dedication Address, July 26 1867, Cheraw," Museum of the Confederacy Archives, Richmond, VA.

38. Robert Seigler, *"Passing the Silent Cup": A Guide to Confederate Monuments in South Carolina* (Columbia: South Carolina Department of Archives and History Press, 1997), 293–94.

39. Palmer, "Ladies Memorial Association, Charleston, South Carolina," in *History of the Confederated Memorial Associations of the South*, 242–43; "Soldiers' National Cemetery," Report of Samuel Weaver to David Willis, esquire agent for A.G. Curtin, governor of Pennsylvania, GNMP, Vertical Files, "Confederate Reinterments," 7-22 PC.

40. Coco, *Strange and Blighted Land*, 80–141.

41. "List of South Carolinians, Who fell at Gettysburg, whose Remains have been, Removed to Magnolia Cemetery, by the, Ladies Memorial Association, of Charleston, S.C.," GNMP, Vertical File, "Charleston Ladies' Memorial Association of South Carolina Re-interments," 7-23 PC. Some records state that only 74 South Carolinians were returned to Magnolia Cemetery. Meanwhile, North Carolina and Georgia joined the effort to repatriate the remains from their states to Raleigh and Atlanta, respectively. Finally, in 1873, the Richmond LMA decided to

rebury all remains (2,273 soldiers) that could be found on the Gettysburg battlefield at Hollywood Cemetery in a "Gettysburg Section."

42. Gregory Coco, "Where Defeated Valor Lies"; "List of South Carolinians, Who fell at Gettysburg, whose Remains have been, Removed to Magnolia Cemetery, by the, Ladies Memorial Association, of Charleston, S.C.," GNMP, Vertical File, "Charleston Ladies' Memorial Association of South Carolina Re-interments," 7-23 PC. It is unlikely that William Daniel's body was returned to his family in South Carolina prior to 1871. His brother, James, of the Seventh South Carolina Infantry, was also killed at the Battle of Gettysburg and his remains were not returned to South Carolina. It should be assumed that the family would claim both bodies if they claimed one. However, although James's body was listed on the O'Neal roster and was still marked into the 1870s, his body was not taken with the South Carolinians in 1871. Instead, his body was not returned to the South until 1873, when he was reburied in Richmond's Hollywood Cemetery.

43. Dr. J. Dickson Bruns, "Ode," in *Confederate Memorial Day, Charleston, S.C., Reinterment of the Carolina Dead from Gettysburg, Address of Rev. Dr. Girardeau, Odes, &c.* (Charleston: William G. Mazyck, 1871), 4–5; Palmer, "Ladies Memorial Association, Charleston, South Carolina," in *History of the Confederate Memorial Associations of the South*, 242; Seigler, *Guide to Confederate Monuments*, 111; Charleston *News and Courier*, December 1, 1882. The newspaper account errs by stating that the Confederate dead from Gettysburg were reburied in Magnolia in 1870. The actual date was 1871.

44. Reverend John L. Girardeau, "Address," in *Confederate Memorial Day, Charleston, S.C., Reinterment of the Carolina Dead from Gettysburg*, 7.

45. Ibid., 17.

46. *Confederate Memorial Day, Charleston, S.C., Reinterment of the Carolina Dead from Gettysburg*, 13, 22–31.

47. Palmer, "Ladies Memorial Association, Charleston, South Carolina," in *History of the Confederate Memorial Associations of the South*, 242.

48. Alexander, "Visiting Manassas Battlefield," 380.

CHAPTER 3

49. *Port Royal New South*, November 21, 1863.

50. Ibid.; Willie Lee Rose, *Rehearsal for Reconstruction: The Port Royal Experiment* (Indianapolis: The Bobbs-Merrill Company, Inc., 1964), xv–xvi.

51. National Cemetery Administration, "Burial and Memorial Benefits: General History," http://www.cem.va.gov/cem/hist_histhome.asp;

NOTES TO PAGES 46–49

National Cemetery Administration, "History of Government Furnished Headstones and Markers," http://www.cem.va.gov/cem/hist/hmhist. asp.

52. Abraham Lincoln, *The Collected Works of Abraham Lincoln*, 6, ed. Roy P. Basler (New Brunswick, NJ: Rutgers University Press, 1953), 98; *Beaufort Free South*, January 10, 1863. Abram D. Smith was incorrectly listed as "A.C. Smith" on Lincoln's official order. Some primary sources list the purchasing date of the Polly's Grove parcel as March 11, 1863, whereas others list it as February 11, 1863.

53. Rose, *Rehearsal for Reconstruction*, xv–xvi, 202–79.

54. Whitman, "Remarks on National Cemeteries," 226.

55. David Charles Sloane, *The Last Great Necessity: Cemeteries in American History* (Baltimore: Johns Hopkins University Press, 1991), 44–64; Gerhard Spieler, "Dixonville Dates Back to Reconstruction," *Beaufort Gazette*, March 30, 2003; Gary Laderman, *The Sacred Remains: American Attitudes Toward Death, 1799–1883* (New Haven: Yale University Press, 1996), 96–107; Colin Brooker, "The North-West Quadrant, Beaufort, South Carolina: A Preliminary History, 1710–1880," report prepared for Historic Beaufort Foundation, Beaufort, SC, 1999.

56. Sloane, *The Last Great Necessity*, 97–99.

57. Department of Veterans Affairs, National Cemetery Administration, *Beaufort National Cemetery*, handout, 2004; James McPherson, *For Cause and Comrades: Why Men Fought in the Civil War* (New York: Oxford University Press, 1997). This semicircular cemetery design was also used at Antietam National Cemetery (1862), Gettysburg National Cemetery (1863) and various other national cemeteries established during the Civil War. Most Confederates utilized pastoral cemetery design when they developed their cemeteries in the postwar years but did not bury their dead in the semicircular arrangement. One noteworthy Confederate semicircular cemetery is the Confederate cemetery at Antietam.

58. National Cemetery Administration, "Burial and Memorial Benefits: General History"; National Cemetery Administration, "Veterans Benefits and Services: Burial and Memorial Benefits"; Rose, *Rehearsal for Reconstruction*, 279–83.

59. National Cemetery Administration, "Burial and Memorial Benefits: General History"; National Cemetery Administration, "Veterans Benefits and Services: Burial and Memorial Benefits"; Rose, *Rehearsal for Reconstruction*, 279–83; Civil War Interment Records, Beaufort National Cemetery, ed. Martin H. Baldwin, http://www.angelfire.com/sc/ historysc/bncc.html.

60. Ester Hill Hawks, *A Woman Doctor's Civil War: Ester Hill Hawks' Diary*, ed. Gerald Schwartz (Columbia: University of South Carolina Press, 1984) 47–48; *Beaufort Free South*, July 25, 1863, and August 29, 1863; *Port Royal New South*, August 8, 1863. *Beaufort Free South* actually lists the USCT hospital as General Hospital #6.

61. R.O. Tyler, Quartermaster's Report on March 12, 1868, Records of the National Cemetery; Gerhard Spieler, "Beaufort's National Cemetery," undated clipping, history file, Beaufort National Cemetery.

62. National Cemetery Administration, *Beaufort National Cemetery*, handout; Civil War Interment Records, Beaufort National Cemetery, ed. Martin H. Baldwin; Spieler, "Beaufort's National Cemetery," Records of the National Cemetery. There are also six citizens buried in the national cemetery in standard Confederate graves. Although several of the graves have wartime death dates, no records remain to ascertain more about these burials. Three of the men buried in this section are marked as working in the Quartermaster's Department and records indicate that they were with the Union army. This information conflicts with the tombstones, which are decidedly of Confederate design, with pointed tops and the Confederate Cross of Honor.

63. Civil War Interment Records, Beaufort National Cemetery, ed. Martin H. Baldwin; Basler, *Lincoln*, 98.

64. Rose, *Rehearsal for Reconstruction*, 202–79.

65. *Port Royal New South*, April 18, 1863.

66. R.O. Tyler, Quartermaster's Report on March 12, 1868, Records of the National Cemetery; Whitman, "Remarks on National Cemeteries," 232. From March 1863 until May 1868, there are no records or newspaper articles remaining to document what planning occurred at the national cemetery or who was involved in the planning. However, W.E. Wording's signature appears on documents in 1868, which indicates that the original land purchasing agents had influence in the development of the national cemetery. Based on correspondence from the U.S. Attorney General's Office and the Quartermaster's Department, Sergeant R.O. Tyler assumed control of Beaufort National Cemetery during 1868.

67. Whitman, "Remarks on National Cemeteries," 235; R.O. Tyler, Quartermaster's Report on March 12, 1868, Records of the National Cemetery; letter from the U.S. Attorney General's Office, March 25, 1869, Records of the National Cemetery; indenture from D.J. Corbin, U.S. District Attorney's Office, April 10, 1868, Records of the National Cemetery; Niels Christensen, Christensen Family Papers, South Caroliniana Library, University of South Carolina, Columbia.

68. Christensen Family Papers; Monica Maria Tetzlaff, *Cultivating a New South: Abbie Holmes Christensen and the Politics of Race and Gender, 1852–1938* (Columbia: University of South Carolina Press, 2002); Whitman, "Remarks on National Cemeteries," 235; National Cemetery Administration, "Veterans Benefits and Services: Burial and Memorial Benefits," http://www.cem.va.gov.

69. Christensen, Landscaping Inventories, Christensen Family Papers; Tetzlaff, *Cultivating a New South*, 136–39. Mrs. Abbie Holmes Christensen, Mrs. R.B. French and Mrs. R.R. Legare were three important patrons of the cemetery's internal improvements. Officially, the Port Royal Agricultural School was not established until November 4, 1901, according to fundraising pamphlets located in the Christensen Family Papers. Yet inventories of plants purchased for the national cemetery in the 1870s clearly mention the Port Royal Agricultural School. It is possible that the Christensens operated a forerunner to the later and better-known school of the 1900s.

70. Christensen, Landscaping Inventories, Christensen Family Papers. Evidence of Christensen's landscaping is also still evident in the municipal Evergreen Cemetery. Magnolia trees, live oaks, azaleas and other plants in Evergreen Cemetery match those planted in the national cemetery. However, there is no discernable pattern linking the landscaping of Evergreen Cemetery to the national cemetery's semicircle.

71. *Port Royal New South*; *Beaufort Republican*; Records of the National Cemetery; R.O. Tyler, Quartermaster's Report on March 12, 1868, Records of the National Cemetery; Michael Vlach, *Back of the Big House: The Architecture of Plantation Slavery* (Chapel Hill: University of North Carolina Press, 1993).

72. William W. Belknap, "Beaufort National Cemetery," *Report on the Inspection of the National Cemeteries, 1870–1871*, 42nd Congress, 2nd Session, Executive Document No. 79; Laura Matilda Towne, *Letters and Diary of Laura M. Towne: Written from the Sea Islands of South Carolina, 1862–1884*, ed. Rupert Sargent Holland (New York: Negro University Press, 1969), 294–95.

73. Citizens' Petition Protesting Christensen's Removal, Presented to Major General Montgomery Meigs, Christensen Family Papers. Although the archival folder states that the letter is circa 1875, other documentation in the Christensen Family Papers reveals that Christensen was still on the government payroll in 1876. Therefore, Christensen was probably dismissed from his position in mid- to late 1876. In this folder, there is a partial letter demanding the removal of W.F. Sanders. Sanders most

likely served as superintendent of Beaufort National Cemetery for a short period of time following Christensen's removal.

74. *Beaufort Republican,* June 5, 1873, and July 10, 1863.

75. *Beaufort Tribune* and *Port Royal Commercial,* May 31, 1877.

76. Ellery M. Brayton, *An address delivered on Decoration Day, May 30, 1890, at the National Cemetery, Beaufort, S.C.*; William R.A. Palmer, *Colored soldiers in the Civil War: address delivered at National Cemetery, Beaufort, S.C., before citizens and G.A.R., May 30th, 1896, also before Epworth League chapters, of the Denmark circuit, Decoration day, May 30th, 1897.*

77. Towne, *Letters and Diary of Laura M. Towne,* 294–95; George Brown Tindall, *South Carolina Negroes: 1877–1900* (Columbia: University of South Carolina Press, 1952), 289–90.

78. Speiler, "Beaufort National Cemetery," Records of the National Cemetery; Donna P. Harris, e-mail message to author, November 16, 2004.

79. Whitman, "Remarks on National Cemeteries," 238.

CHAPTER 4

80. Charleston *News and Courier,* May 14, 1879. Reprinted in South Carolina Monument Association, *Origin, History and Work with An Account of the Proceedings at the Unveiling of the Monument to the Confederate Dead, and the Oration of Gen. John S. Preston, at Columbia, S.C., May 13, 1879* (Charleston: The News and Courier Book Press, 1879).

81. Ibid.

82. The Sumter County monument was constructed earlier than the State House monument, as its base was dedicated in 1874 and the monument completed in 1875 (although the monument says 1876). The monument was located in a prominent position in front of the "Washington School," which was a privately funded public school. In 1897, when the monument transferred from the LMA to the UDC, the land was also leased to the City of Sumter. Therefore, initially the monument was on private property, even though today it is considered more public land. Furthermore, the monument might have been altered later in its history, about 1888. This seems very plausible, as its front and inscription of all of the soldiers from Sumter County are reflective of a later time period. Seigler, *Guide to Confederate Monuments,* 476–81; "Sumter," February 4, 1957, CMMSC.

83. "South Carolina Monument," *Confederate Veteran* 8 (1899): 231–32; contract, "Between the South Carolina Monument Association and Muldoon & Co., Agreement," August 1, 1873, Confederate Monument

Series, SCCRRMM; Seigler, *Guide to Confederate Monuments*, 216–21; "Confederate Monument at Columbia," *Confederate Veteran* 15 (1907): 127.

84. "South Carolina Monument," *Confederate Veteran* 8 (1899): 231–32; South Carolina Monument Association, *Origin, History and Work*.

85. Undated ledger of the South Carolina Monuments Association, Confederate Monuments Series, SCCRRMM.

86. South Carolina Monument Association, *Origin, History and Work*, 52–65.

87. After the monument was struck by lightning, the original monument's head and hand were sent to the South Carolina Room at the Confederate Memorial Literary Society in Richmond, now known as the Museum of the Confederacy. The monument pieces remained on display through the early years of the museum, but the head has since gone missing from the collection. The hand is still in the possession of the Museum of the Confederacy. "Soldier's Head Not the Same as on Original," *The State*, November 8, 1959, from CMMSC scrapbook, SCCRRMM; "Whom Defeat Could Not Dishonor," *The State Magazine*, May 11, 1952, 6–7; "South Carolina Monument," *Confederate Veteran* 8 (1899): 231–32.

88. Supposedly, the face on the first monument was taken from a photograph of a soldier from Beaufort who was killed during the war. "Soldier's Head Not the Same as on Original," *The State*.

89. "First Annual Meeting Survivors' Association of the State of South Carolina," reprinted letter dated 12 August 1869, Charleston Museum Archives.

90. Steve Davis, "Empty Eyes, Marble Hand: The Confederate Monument and the South," *Journal of Popular Culture* 16 (Winter 1982): 7.

91. South Carolina Monument Association, *Origin, History and Work*, 7–8.

92. Palmer, "Ladies Memorial Association, Charleston, South Carolina," in *History of the Confederated Memorial Associations of the South*, 242.

93. Charleston *News and Courier*, December 1, 1882.

94. Ibid.

95. Ibid.

96. Ibid.

97. Julia F. Schouboe, "Florence Memorial Association," Confederate Monument Series, SCCRRMM.

98. Seigler, *Guide to Confederate Monuments*, 358–61.

99. Ibid.

100. Ibid.

101. Reverend John Kershaw, "Address Delivered Before the Ladies' Memorial Association and Citizens of Charleston on Memorial Day, May

10, 1893, by the Rev. John Kershaw" (Charleston: The Daggett Printing Co., 1893), 4–5, Confederate Monuments Series, SCCRRMM.

CHAPTER 5

102. A Student of Sculpture, "About 'Kind of Monument to Erect,'" *Confederate Veteran* 16 (1908): xii.

103. Ibid.

104. Rutherford, "History of the Ladies Memorial Associations," 11.

105. Palmer, "Ladies Memorial Association, Charleston, South Carolina," in *History of the Confederated Memorial Associations of the South*, 244.

106. Elmwood Cemetery Correspondence, Elmwood Cemetery Record Series, SCCRRMM.

107. Seigler, *Guide to Confederate Monuments*, 370–72, 411–13.

108. "Ceremonies at the Unveiling of the South Carolina Monument on the Chickamauga Battlefield," 39.

109. Not everyone fully bought into the reconciliation speech, and in many ways it was only the first layer of healing on a deep wound. In 1902, a group of Confederate veterans in Virginia attempted to erect a monument in Richmond to Grant. The fund only managed to raise sixteen dollars. That same year, a man in New Jersey attempted a similarly unsuccessful campaign to erect a monument to Grant and Lee. The soldiers, wives and children of the Civil War generation took longer in actually adopting aspects of reconciliation and nationalism into their lives. Michael Kammen, *Mystic Cords of Memory: The Transformation of Tradition in American Culture* (New York: Knopf, 1991), 109.

110. Richard Rollins, *The Returned Battle Flags* (Redondo Beach, CA: Rank and File Publications, 1995), iii; "Marking Confederate Graves in the North," *Confederate Veteran* 15 (1907): 539.

111. Seigler, *Guide to Confederate Monuments*, 386–88.

112. Confederated Southern Memorial Association, "A Message to Memorial Women," *Confederate Veteran* 16 (1918): 228; United Daughters of the Confederacy, "From the President General," *Confederate Veteran* 16 (1918): 316.

113. Elizabeth Waring McMaster, *Girls of the Sixties* (Columbia, SC: The State Company, 1937), 5–10; "The Girls of the Sixties," *The State*, July 11, 1937.

114. Ana Carden-Coyne, "Wounded Visionaries," November 13, 2008, available at http://www.guardian.co.uk. Article is an excerpt from her upcoming book *Reconstructing the Body: Classicism, Modernism and the First*

World War, to be published by Oxford University Press in the summer of 2009.

115. "Memorial Fountain at St. Matthews, S.C.," *Confederate Veteran* 32 (1924): 359.

116. "The Virginians of the Valley," by Francis Orrery Ticknor, inscription on the grave of Major General Matthew C. Butler, Old Village Cemetery (Willowbrook Cemetery), Edgefield, South Carolina.

CHAPTER 6

117. Mrs. L.P. Fulp, "Ladies' Confederate Memorial Association, Fort Mill, South Carolina," in *History of the Confederated Memorial Association*, 244–46.

118. Louise Pettus, "Confederate Statue—Fort Mill," *York Observer*, August 21, 188.

119. Mrs. J.M. Riddle, "Report of Lancaster Chapter UDC," October 29, 1909, unpublished, SCCRRMM; "South Carolina's Tribute to Her Women: How the Large Sum was Procured," *Confederate Veteran* 20 (1912): 243–44; Pettus, "Confederate Statue—Fort Mill," *York Observer*, August 21, 1988.

120. "Catawba Indians Will Be Remembered," *The State*, August 1, 1900. Transcribed by Paul R. Sarrett Jr., August 11, 1998. Available USGenWeb Archives Project, online. Sent to the author by Louise Pettus.

121. Fulp, "Fort Mill, South Carolina," in *History of the Confederated Memorial Association*, 244–46.

122. "Catawba Indians Will Be Remembered," *The State*, August 1, 1900.

123. "South Carolina's Tribute to Her Women," *Confederate Veteran* 20 (1912): 243–44.

124. *The State*, April 12, 1912; Seigler, *Guide to Confederate Monuments*, 225–30.

125. "South Carolina's Tribute to Her Women," *Confederate Veteran*, 243–44.

126. Ribbon from Wade Hampton's grave with description, SCCRRMM Collection; Seigler, *Guide to Confederate Monuments*, 222–24.

127. Seigler, *Guide to Confederate Monuments*, 222–24.

128. Ibid., 94–98.

129. Ibid.

130. Smithsonian American Art Museum's Inventories of American Painting and Sculpture, online database available at http://siris-artinventories.si.edu.

131. Grave of John J. McKain, Quaker Cemetery, Camden, South Carolina.

132. Grave of Colonel Thomas Glascock Bacon, Old Village Cemetery (Willowbrook Cemetery), Edgefield, South Carolina.

CHAPTER 7

133. "Unveiling of the South Carolina Monument on the Chickamauga Battlefield," 23–24.

134. Lizzie George Henderson, "Appeal for Monuments and Markers," *Confederate Veteran* 14 (1906): 164–65; News clipping, "Grand Army of the Republic," research file, GNMP; Sanford Levison, *Written in Stone: Public Monuments in Changing Societies* (Durham and London: Duke University Press, 1998), 42.

135. "Unveiling of the South Carolina Monument on the Chickamauga Battlefield," 44–45; Smithsonian American Art Museum's Inventories of American Painting and Sculpture.

136. "Unveiling of the South Carolina Monument on the Chickamauga Battlefield," 36–38.

137. Ibid., 38–39.

138. Ibid., 23.

139. Harlan D. Unrau, *Administrative History: Gettysburg National Military Park and Cemetery, Pennsylvania*, United States Department of the Interior, National Park Service, July 1991.

140. Ibid., 46, 67.

141. Ibid., 63.

142. David G. Martin, *Confederate Monuments at Gettysburg: The Gettysburg Battle Monuments* (Hightstown, NJ: Longstreet House, 1986), 1:1–28; Unrau, *Administrative History: Gettysburg National Military Park and Cemetery*, 68–77.

143. Unrau, *Administrative History: Gettysburg National Military Park and Cemetery*, 93–94.

144. Martin, *Confederate Monuments at Gettysburg*, 1:1–28.

145. Ibid.

146. Ralph W. Widener Jr., *Confederate Monuments: Enduring Symbols of the South and the War Between the States* (Ralph W. Widener Jr., 1982).

147. Brigadier General Samuel McGowan Camp 40, Laurens, SC, "McGowan's Brigade Monument," available at http://mcgowansbrigademonument.awardspace.com. Further information about the project was provided by Gary Davis and Robert Roper III through e-mail correspondence in January 2009.

148. "Unveiling of the South Carolina Monument on the Chickamauga Battlefield," 23–24.

CONCLUSION

149. Adams, "Tales of a Grandmother, or, Recollections of the Confederate War," in *South Carolina Women in the Confederacy*, 210–11.

150. Charleston *News and Courier*, May 14, 1879.

151. "Unveiling of the South Carolina Monument on the Chickamauga Battlefield," 25.

INDEX

INDEX

Please visit us at
www.historypress.net